What Others Are Saying About You Are Beautiful...

"I found *You Are Beautiful* to be like a love letter to Jesus, with all the joy, sensitivity, and warmth that such a penning would be expected to elicit. Its mixture of personal testimony, anecdote, and beautiful exegesis of scripture is both thought provoking and spiritually challenging and stimulating. It can be read in one sitting, or as a daily meditation. I'm *joy*fully looking at life with a bit more excitement and anticipation than I did before I read this book."

—**Gillette Elvgren,** Ph.D.
Professor
Communication and Theatre Arts
Regent University

D1566262

"Dr. Joy Francis has written a powerful book that will minister to the hearts of scores of women who desire to hear from their heavenly Father that they are valuable, cherished, and loved. Her heart for the Lord, as well as for women and children, is evident on every page. Her message will find fertile soil in the lives of women who desire to become all that God has created them to be. Further, her desire to contribute to the eradication of human trafficking, especially of young children, should strike a resonating chord within all of us. I highly commend her book, which provides deep glimpses into the Father's heart."

—**Diane J. Chandler,** Ph.D.
Associate Professor
School of Divinity, Regent University

"One of the foremost roles of the Holy Spirit in the life of the believer is the renewing of our minds. Salvation brings an instantaneous new birth of the spirit, but the renewing of the mind is a lifelong and often a challenging process. *You Are Beautiful* presents a blueprint for renewal. The truths recorded on the pages of this book show us how we look through God's eyes, acting as a catalyst to change the way we think about ourselves and our God. This book will accelerate your spiritual growth as a source of inspiration, healing, and wisdom. The personal testimonies found on these pages simply illustrate that God stands

ready to renew the mind of any believer who comes with an open heart, leading to more intimacy with God and greater empowerment in life."
—Dr. James T. Flynn
Associate Professor of Practical Theology
Regent University

"Dr. Joy chooses to experience and share God's love through an unfiltered lens. Her writing seamlessly blends the stories of individuals from scripture with her own stories and those of her students so that we feel she—and us, too—are an integral part of this fabric of faith stretching from the beginning into the never-ending reaches of God's time."
—Liz Hansen
Screenwriter

"Reading *You Are Beautiful* is the chance to sit under the teaching of a woman completely enamored with and delighted by God. Her passion for her Heavenly Father is intoxicating and contagious. Curl up with a cup of tea and this book, and prepare your heart for healing."
—Lacie Wright
Former student and author of *Covenant for Kids!*

"To this day, I still talk about Dr. Joy's impact on my life with my friends and family. In this book, you will read uplifting stories that will make your heart smile and bring tears to your eyes. Dr. Joy: Thank you!"
—Nicole Banwarth
Communications major
Old Dominion University Alum 2007

"Dr. Joy has such a pure heart for Jesus. Anyone who meets her cannot help but see the Lord through her life. This book, *You Are Beautiful*, compels one to remember how intricately God fashioned us for His glory. The simple truths so eloquently written, illustrate the great love that God has for us and His desire for relationship with us."
—Kourtney Ragland Perry
Doctoral of Physical Therapy student
Old Dominion University
Class of 2012

"Inspirational! Just like the author. Every student in her classes leaves it a different person; I know I did. This book just barely scratches the surface on what a truly amazing lady she is!"

—Angela Petroccia
Business Management
Class of 2011

"This book reflects Dr. Joy's wonderful personality, and serves as an encouragement of God's amazing love for us!"

—Natasha Morrison
Former student
Old Dominion University
Class of 2011

"Dr. Joy implements in her own life what she teaches in this book."

—Pastors Melvin and Denise McCleese
New Life Providence Church

"This is a love story about the truest love. Understanding God's love for you is essential and this book really helps it come alive."

—Emily Knollenberg
Biology major
Old Dominion University

"Very eye-opening and inspirational! A great read to help make one feel loved and unique. Written by a professor who cares about her students and inspires them to be their best."

—Kathryn Chappell
Human Service and Psychology
Old Dominion University
Class of 2011

"We live in perilous times, where human brokenness is at an all-time high. Trends in technology and modernization are proving catastrophic to human hearts, from depression and suicide, to the global phenomenon of human trafficking. Dr. Joy's book *You Are Beautiful* is a reminder of a simple truth that is often too easy to forget: we are valuable to God and cherished by Him. If this foundational piece of information is ruptured in a human heart, a thousand expressions of brokenness may follow. Victims of human trafficking have been robbed of this fundamental identity as a child loved by God. The devastation they have endured sends the message that they are forgotten, filthy, and trash. The process of restoration of these victims—and everyone, really, who has suffered loss and hurt—is to introduce an identity rooted in the love of God—one that speaks to them that they are cherished, clean, and extremely precious. Weaving stories with insights from spiritual leaders of our times, Dr. Joy helps us hear what God is speaking in this critical hour."

—Benjamin Nolot
Founder and President,
Exodus Cry
Producer/Director,
Nefarious: Merchant of Souls

You Are Beautiful

You Are Beautiful

A Journey of Discovery

DR. JOY FRANCIS

WinePressPublishing
Great Books, Defined.

© 2011 by Dr. Joy Francis. All rights reserved.

Photographs for the front cover were provided compliments of the artist, Renee Caya.

WinePress Publishing (PO Box 428, Enumclaw, WA 98022) functions only as book publisher. As such, the ultimate design, content, editorial accuracy, and views expressed or implied in this work are those of the author.

No part of this publication may be reproduced, stored in a retrieval system, or transmitted in any way by any means—electronic, mechanical, photocopy, recording, or otherwise—without the prior permission of the copyright holder, except as provided by USA copyright law.

Scripture quotations, unless otherwise notated, are from the *New American Standard Version* of the Bible, © 1960, 1963, 1968, 1971, 1972, 1973, 1975, 1977, 1995 by The Lockman Foundation. Used by permission.. All bold face type within scriptures has been added by the author for emphasis.

ISBN 13: 978-1-4141-1790-4
ISBN 10: 1-4141-1790-6
Library of Congress Catalog Card Number: 2010905927

Make my garden breathe out fragrance,
Let its spices be wafted abroad.
—Song of Solomon 4:16

Contents

⟿⫷⟾

Preface

HER EYES GAZED at me from her brokenness. She yearned for someone to say to her, "You are valuable." Valuable…valuable apart from anything she could do to prove she was worthy of love. Valuable… valuable apart from any gifts or talent she had. Valuable in spite of her marred past. Valuable, even if she did not perform perfectly in her academic endeavors.

As I looked at one of my young students, I longed to convince her of her value in Christ. Observing her plight served as a catalyst as I felt the Lord pressing me to get His message of unconditional love out to others including my students—young and old alike. I had never written a book before, so this was an adventure!

As I wrote through one long, blustery winter, I gazed at a photo of two hands holding several beautiful daisies. It was called "The Offering." That is what this book is to me—the beginning of a journey for me—a journey that would teach me I am valuable, beautiful, cherished, redeemed, forgiven, set apart, pure, and holy.

As I wrote, my heart awakened to the plight of young children around the world. Due to human trafficking and other ills, they fail to know their worth. The proceeds from this book will go to organizations that help children know they are valuable, cared for, and protected by a loving Father.

Knowing that this book would serve two purposes blessed me greatly. For the reader, it will speak words of life and truth that will bring a breakthrough in the reader's life. At the same time, the profits will materially convey a message of intrinsic value to children around the world. The latter is what both inspired and compelled me to finish this book.

Consider this book a love song sung over you. It is one God is singing for you as Zephaniah 3:17 says: "The Lord your God is in your midst, a victorious warrior He will exalt over you with joy, He will be quiet in His love, He will rejoice over you with shouts of joy." It is His heartfelt desire that we may know our value before the Father and know the Father's heart toward us. This book is also a revelation of His character as faithful, just, and sovereign. His role is as your healer, deliverer, comforter, and best friend.

Chapter 1

Redeemed

Yet for this reason I found mercy, so that in me as the foremost, Jesus
Christ might demonstrate His perfect patience as an example for those
who would believe in Him for eternal life.

—1 Tim. 1:16

Surrender

HER HAIR HUNG softly about her as she searched through the sea of
faces to see the one for whom her heart longed. Tentatively, she walked
past the guests until her gaze beheld the one she had been searching for.
Her eyes wet with tears, she knelt before Jesus. "Forgive me, Lord," she
whispered. "I have sinned beyond what I deem salvageable. If I could
just hear Your voice. If You would just mend my heart."

And then, she took it out, her alabaster vial. It was all she had—her
dowry—a full year's wages. "It is Yours," she whispered. Breaking it
open, she poured out its contents before Him, anointing His feet with
oil. "And standing behind Him at his feet, weeping, she began to wet
his feet with her tears, and kept wiping them with the hair of her head,
and kissing His feet and anointing them with the perfume" (Luke 7:38).
Jesus was deeply moved as she washed His feet with this costly, fragrant
perfume. In spite of what others thought, she, through tears, continued
pouring out her fragrant oil and kissing the Lord's feet.

1

"She is a sinner," one of the Pharisees said, gasping. Jesus, knowing the man's heart, was moved with compassion for her. He sought to protect the young woman from ridicule. He gently rebuked the man.

> "A moneylender had two debtors; one owed five hundred denarii, and the other fifty. When they were unable to repay, he graciously forgave them both. So which of them will love him more?"
> Simon answered and said, "I suppose the one whom he forgave more." And He said to him, "You have judged correctly."
> —Luke 7:41-43

Normally, a host offered water for washing to his guests upon their arrival. The roads were very dirty, and it was protocol for a guest to wash his feet upon entering a house. Not only had this courtesy not been extended to Jesus, but His host had not greeted Him with a kiss as He entered the abode. Rather, this woman had washed his feet with her tears, dried them with her hair, and poured out her precious oil upon his feet while kissing them.

Jesus continued, "For this reason, I say to you, her sins, which are many, have been forgiven, for she loved much; but he who is forgiven little, loves little" (Luke 7:47). Gently, He tilted her head so He could gaze into her eyes. "Your sins have been forgiven," He said. "Your faith has saved you; go in peace" (Luke 7:48, 50).

> One who is forgiven much, loves much.

Love had been poured out upon her—extravagant love. Imagine the sweet fragrance that filled the room. Her love was in offering him her heart through this extravagant gift. His love was in later offering her His life on the cross. As she left that place, the aroma lingered.

> How beautiful is your love, my sister, my bride! How much better is your love than wine, and the **fragrance** of your oils than all kinds of spices!
> —Song of Solomon 4:10

You Are Forgiven

Like that of the woman with the fragrant perfume, my story is a simple one. It is a story of restoration and redemption woven into a beautiful tapestry by a Redeemer who set me free, forgave me, and continues to pour His love upon me. It is a story of my grateful heart as I sit at His feet, my eyes ever fixed upon the One who called me out of darkness and into His marvelous light. Breaking my alabaster vase before Him, I surrendered my heart, mind, and will to Him for His remaking.

I remember how I felt when God rescued me...overwhelmed. I sat stunned as peace finally flooded my soul. "You forgive me too, Lord?" I asked, pausing as I tried to take it all in. "I would have been happy if you had just spoken to me again." As I knelt in my living room at His feet, tears streaming down my face, I cried out. Broken and alone in my apartment, I knew He had heard me. He had answered. I closed my eyes and saw myself falling down into a deep pit, but before I reached the bottom, a giant hand reached down and snatched me up.

"He forgives me," I murmured in wonder. How could this be? I had broken His heart by my actions. "He forgives me." As I went to sleep that night, I felt warmth surround me as if someone were holding me tenderly. I was not alone. He was with me. He had rescued and forgiven me, and I would forever be His.

This was the start of my new beginning. His forgiveness was the first step. The rest of my life would be a love story of how God continues to romance me in spite of my many failings. He knows the end from the beginning; He sees us as we are and will be. And He is confident that He will bring us to that place where we are His pure and spotless bride. He assures us that we are *valuable*.

> We are the reward for His sufferings

True Love

Imagine God the Father speaking to His Son before the beginning of creation. Dana Candler posed the question of why the created order came forth. God the Father might have said, "Son, I am going to give

You a great gift." And then there was a pause. "I am going to give You the voluntary love of a human heart." Think about that for a second. Voluntary love. Not robots conditioned to worship, but the voluntary love of a human heart.[1]

Jesus might have looked up expectantly as God continued, "They will choose You," he repeated. "They will choose *You* before they ever see You. But when they do see You, what a glorious day that will be!" I imagine Jesus purposefully locking eyes with Father God, knowing what was in store. What a treasure we are to Him, and what a cost He paid for us.

As we offer Him our hearts, our broken lives, He redeems them, making them into a love song. A pure freshness touches us. First, when the Spirit of God saves us, we truly become new creatures in Christ. The old passes away; the new comes. We are given a clean slate, yet sometimes we feel so undeserving of it. "After all the wrong I have done, Lord?" we murmur. That is one of the mysteries of His majesty, and one to be discussed in later chapters.

> "For we are a fragrance of Christ to God among those who are being saved and among those who are perishing."
> —2 Cor. 2:15

RECONCILED

I recall hearing at a remarkable Sunday service I attended, a stirring testimony of one man's salvation. David, a gentleman visiting from New Zealand, was in his mid-sixties at the time. In his twenties he had come to know Christ through a miraculous set of circumstances. It is one more testimony of how a loving God pursues us and overwhelms us with His love and forgiveness.

After trying all that the world could give him, David was swimming near a beautiful desert island when he received what should have been a fatal sting by a Man-o-War. By some miracle, David got to shore and called out to the natives for help. Confused as to his request, his slurred speech, and the language barrier, no one called for medical personnel for a full fifteen to twenty minutes. Gradually, his body began to shut down from the poison. As they loaded him into the ambulance bound for a hospital, his limbs grew numb.

Realizing that he was about to die, this hardened young man cried out to God, longing to hear His voice. It was like a game of Russian roulette now. He had sampled everything: Buddhism, Hinduism, New Age, and the like, searching for the meaning of life. Suddenly, his mother's face appeared before him. She was a devout Christian who had been praying for him for years. *If anyone has this thing right, it would be my mom*, he thought. So he asked, "What must I do, God?" And the Lord showed him that he needed to forgive those who had refused to help him as he lay dying on the beach. Angered, at first, David gradually surrendered his desire for vengeance and asked for help in doing this. During the ride, God continued to show him three others whom he needed to forgive.

The ambulance attendant looked down at him grimly, checking the instruments. Gradually every limb began to feel cold; this feeling moved up his legs and arms toward his vital organs. David knew he didn't have much time. "I surrender to You, God. To You, Jesus." Finally, he became completely numb and everything went black.

He opened his eyes and looked around. Where was he? He felt himself in some awful dark place with demonic voices whispering all around him. They got closer...ever closer. Fear gripped him. What was this place? Just as the voices crowded close around him, a brilliant light shone. "Not this one!" he heard a voice full of authority say. And then David felt himself floating to a strange and amazing place.

Before David stood the most beautiful man he had ever seen. The man, robed in white, came to him. His love and purity was so intense that this newly saved young man felt unworthy. "You don't understand all that I have done, Lord." He felt himself unclean and impure. He wanted to run or look away, but he couldn't. Endless waves of love began to envelop him—wave upon wave hit him. The Lord met each accusing thought of unworthiness with tenderness and affirmation. "I am unworthy," was met with, "I love you." "Don't look at me, Lord." "I long to look at you. Turn your face toward me, son." "No, Lord. You don't know all that I have done!" Gently another wave of love swept over him. Jesus said, "I see you. I know all of it and I forgive you. I forgive you. Come to me."

Gradually David turned his gaze upon the One who had loved him with an everlasting love. The light was all encompassing. "I love you," he replied. So overwhelming was this love that his entire being longed to leap and shout for joy. He felt free! He longed to run, skipping throughout this new kingdom he belonged to, to embrace the One who died to save him. He now began to understand this on the other side of eternity.

And then the Lord pointed to something behind him. "What is this?" he wondered. Glancing around, David saw his mother, who, until she reached heaven, would never know that he had been saved by grace through faith. Other relatives who did not yet know the truth leading to salvation were there as well. He turned back to face Jesus, who looked with longing at those souls. Suddenly David knew he was being sent back. "No!" he involuntarily cried, not wishing to leave this place of eternal love. "Yes, my child. You must return that the world may know."

Suddenly, David felt himself back in a hospital bed. A doctor was prodding his legs and feet. One of David's eyes popped open. A nurse just coming into the room, fainted. Another nurse, upon witnessing the opening of one of David's eyes, dropped all of the instruments on her tray. The doctor was stunned, and he believed that perhaps his probing had struck a nerve, causing this response.

David appealed, "Help me, Lord." The strength seemed drained from him. Nothing had moved but that eye. Then the other eye slowly opened, and gradually his body began to revive and he could sit up straight and speak. The nurses and the doctor were shocked! This man had been dead for more than fifteen minutes! The testimony David would later give over the years brought many to Christ, including his whole family. Before she reached heaven, David's mother could rejoice that her son knew the Son of God!

> When you were dead in your transgressions and the uncircumcision of your flesh, He made you alive together with Him, having forgiven us all our transgressions, having canceled out the certificate of debt consisting of decrees against us, which was hostile to us; and He has taken it out of the way, having nailed it to the cross.
> —Col. 2:13-14

OF GREAT VALUE

> As far as the east is from the west, so far has He removed our transgressions from us.
>
> —Ps. 103:12

David, in those first few moments of being a believer in Christ, experienced pangs of guilt and shame. For the first time, he saw his own sin. And yet, Jesus dismissed his every objection and overcame it with a new wave of love. As we learn in the Book of Romans, "But God demonstrates His own love toward us, in that while we were yet sinners, Christ died for us" (Rom. 5:8).

Understanding that we are loved and cherished is a dizzying concept to grasp, even after we come to saving faith in Christ. Yet it is true. Jesus shed His blood and laid down His life for you. He bore everything on that cross with gladness in His heart knowing that it would purchase eternity with you. Jesus "who for the joy set before Him endured the cross" (Heb. 12:2). That is how dear you are to Him! He knew from the beginning that this must take place, and He gave this gift freely… each precious drop of His blood.

Sometimes we feel so mired down by sin, we feel it difficult to stand. We think, *I am so unworthy! Why would anyone, let alone God, love me?* We question why a holy and beautiful God would desire us.

When Jesus looks at us, He doesn't see the darkness or rebellion of our hearts. He sees an immature heart longing to honor Him, willing to follow Him. "The spirit is willing, but the flesh is weak" (Matt. 26:41). I reflect on the life of David, king of Israel, who was called "a man after God's own heart" (Acts 13:22). He sinned with Bathsheba, but he was forgiven when he turned and repented before the Lord. In his series on the Song of Solomon, Mike Bickle elaborates on this very idea.

> "I am dark but lovely."
> *Song of Solomon 1:5*

This is an important discovery to make. God loves us even in our weakness. He is not shocked. He sees the depth and darkness of our hearts, which do not surprise Him. Yet even in our fallen humanity, He sees us through the eyes of love. When He fixes His gaze of love upon us, part of us might long to run away. "Do not stare at me because I am swarthy, for the sun has burned me" (Song of Solomon 1:6). We may feel weighed down by our own sin and wonder what He sees beyond it.

> He loves us even in our weakness.

I know the end of the story, and this is not the end of the story.

—Misty Edwards, IHOP

Chapter 2

Falling in Love

Faith is the assurance of things hoped for, the conviction of things not seen.

—Heb. 11:1

TRAVELING MERCIES

IT WAS MIDNIGHT as I set off into the mountains of Colorado. I always enjoy traveling after dark. There is seldom any traffic, and you have a sense that the precious sunlight or the fresh air of day was not wasted.

Heading west to visit friends, I had about a fourteen-hour drive ahead of me. Full of faith, having just given my life to Christ a year earlier, I had moved to Colorado after finishing college. I believed a new chapter of life was about to begin.

Sunrise was always the hardest part of the drive. It was the time I really felt sleepy. As I rounded the bend about three in the morning, I saw an amazing sight! Before me, *deer were scattered everywhere across the road.* With only seconds before impact, I quickly prayed, "JESUS!!!!! Help me!!!!"

What happened next was a miracle. It was as if Jesus were riding beside me in the passenger seat. I saw a light envelop my car and, suddenly, I had peace. I felt God steering my car for me. Afterwards, my mind reeled, "WOW!" I thought. "Did we pass through them?" My car made it past the deer without a scratch! Breathing hard and now fully awake, I gazed out into the velvet black sky dotted with stars and said, "Thank You," to Him with all my heart.

I fell in love with Him so completely. So faithfully, He kindled and cared for the embers of my love. My early travels were the beginning of an incredible love story.

YOUR BEST FRIEND

> Truly I say to you, if you have faith and do not doubt, you will not only do what was done to this fig tree, but even if you say to this mountain, "Be taken up and cast into the sea," it will happen. And all things you ask in prayer, **believing**, you will receive.
>
> —Matt. 21:21

As I said before, whenever I traveled by car in Colorado, I always felt the presence of the Lord with me. In fact, I routinely joked with my family that I took extended trips just to spend time alone with Jesus. I have many fond memories of driving under resplendent reddish-orange rock arches that curved perfectly with the road and over lesser-known roads at the peak of autumn. If only I had mounted a camera on the roof of my car, I would now have the most stunning photos of deserts, mountains, and lakes.

Back in the old days before the sophisticated weather channels that we have today, I simply picked up a map and went. It never occurred to me to check the weather or to factor it into my planning. Knowing the destination of my next trip, a co-worker mentioned, "Whatever you do, do not go through Bear Creek Pass at this time of year." She said this so solemnly that I pulled out my map, but for the life of me, I could not find Bear Creek Pass. Shrugging, I called my grandfather to let him know I would be traveling and as always, my family prayed for a safe journey.

Faith was an integral part of my life even then. I believed that if God had called me to go somewhere, He would take care of me on the journey. I was confident that the Lord would see me through. He had always been faithful. I was amazed by His love and care for me. At times,

I thought my heart would burst from the pure joy of receiving His love. He had been doing miracles to show me His love since the beginning of my commitment to follow Him. I remembered well the day this broken vessel gave her heart to Him. My faith in His love was unshakable.

It was January as I traveled the southwest route through the mountains and the Four Corners. Having previously travelled on I-25 on another trip, I chose this time to take a more scenic and perhaps shorter route. Although Colorado could be cold where I lived, Boulder did not receive huge amounts of snow. It never occurred to me that I might encounter a great deal of it en route to Arizona.

Climbing higher and higher into the mountains, I marveled at the beauty surrounding me. Light snow began to gently fall around my car. Beautiful pine trees, gracing the sides of the road, seemed to whisper to me. There was a majestic hush all around. Still full of faith, I did not worry.

But where am I? I wondered. There had been no signs for forty-five minutes since the flashing one stating, "No Chains Needed Today." "Chains," I had repeated, still a novice driver, "for cars?" I had not seen another car for some time. The wind began to blow snow directly across the road. I was in the mountains now. If I had stopped and stepped outside my car, I would have seen I was on top of one! Glancing at the map, I pondered if I had enough gas to return the way I had come. Then I saw it. To my right, a sign clearly read, "Bear Creek Pass." My eyes grew wide in wonder. Above me people rode ski lifts up the mountains toward a lodge.

I began to laugh, thinking of what my friend had told me. Bear Creek Pass was normally impassable this time of year. "No Chains Today," I muttered. By some miracle it had been passable today and I did not have to double back and travel an hour and a half. Still, the road ahead was treacherous. I remember the moment the ice and snow began to thaw. It was as if the seasons changed before my very eyes.

As I came around a bend in the road, the purity of the white, clean snow shifted once again into the colorful leaves of autumn I had encountered on the other side of the pass. It was a gradual transition. There was grass, and the roads were gray asphalt rather than snow-packed. "Thank You, Lord," I whispered gratefully and let out a long sigh of relief. Once more I had been rescued by the love of an awesome Father. I was filled with faith.

> Because he has loved Me, therefore I will deliver him; I will set him securely on high, because he has known My name. He will call upon Me, and I will answer him; I will be with him in trouble; I will rescue him and honor him."
>
> —Ps. 91:14-15

ONE MORE FOR THE ROAD

"If you can?" All things are possible to him who believes.

—Mark 9:23

Taking a leap of faith sometimes feels like jumping onto the invisible bridge in an *Indiana Jones* movie. Yet, time and time again, when I have jumped, God has caught me. God is faithful. We are not to test God, but to listen to Him and obey.

As I journeyed to Phoenix, I pondered my future. I was interviewing to teach at a local Montessori school. Having just graduated from college, and interested in home schooling my children one day, I was also investigating the University of Phoenix's graduate program in education.

It was a long, arduous drive. Eighteen hours straight. Being young and fearless, eighteen hours was just about right for me. I chose not to stay in hotels en route purely for financial reasons.

Driving through the desert, I saw a sign that said, "No Gas for 120 Miles," as I entered an Indian reservation, I glanced at my fuel gauge. The tank was full as I had just recently filled up. A dusty red horizon greeted me as I drove beneath majestic arches and around rocks beautifully carved by the wind. I smiled, thinking, "More Jesus time."

All went well until about the sixteenth hour. It was early evening now. As I crossed into Flagstaff, it began to rain torrentially. My windshield wipers could not handle the rain. Then, lightning cracked in the sky, and in an instant all highway lights disappeared. Even with my headlights, *I could barely see the road ahead!*

I edged over to the median and literally followed it. If I had pulled over and put on my hazard lights, I might have been hit. In a fierce rainstorm like this one, my car could have been mistaken for a moving car. I proceeded with caution. To further complicate the problem, I was wearing prescription sunglasses. As I rolled down the window, the rain pelted my face. At that moment, I comically wished for sunglass wipers. It was now raining so hard that I could only see the exit signs as I passed them.

At that instant, another car pulled onto the freeway. No one else was driving on the road. It was as if that car had been sent to guide me on my way. I followed its tail lights until the rain began to dissipate. Then, just when I was safe, the car ahead of me gracefully exited the freeway.

I marveled. God had been with me through the rain. An hour and half later, I crawled into a dorm bed at the University of Phoenix and drifted off to sleep.

When I called my mom the next morning to let her know I had arrived safely, she asked, "What happened to you last night?"

"Why?" I replied curiously.

"Well, I was asleep and I had this vision of you dead on the side of the road. So, I awoke and began to pray," she said.

"What time was this?" I questioned. It turned out to be the exact time that I had been praying on the road in the rain. Once again, God had protected me.

> For He will give His angels charge concerning you, to guard you in all your ways. They will bear you up in their hands, that you do not strike your foot against a stone.
>
> —Ps. 91:11-12

ANGELS AMONG US?

> Do not neglect to show hospitality to strangers, for by this some have entertained angels without knowing it.
>
> —Heb. 13:2

Her name was Angel. She was interviewing at the same time I was for a position at a Montessori school in Phoenix. Walking through the school with her on a tour, I felt some confusion and disorganization about the school. Newly graduated from college, I had been hopeful about a prospective move to Arizona.

After the interview, Angel invited me to lunch. I had reservations about the Montessori school, but had been afraid to voice them. Angel, who was very good with numbers, quickly calculated what our earnings would be at the school. She crunched the numbers in her calculator, thoughtfully subtracting the taxes. When it was all said and done, my pay would be significantly less than what I was currently making in Colorado. I was not very knowledgeable about finances up to that point.

Everything I needed to know, God had answered or confirmed in that conversation. Angel and I went on to talk about the structure of the school, the rigorous work schedule, and the high cost of living in Phoenix. That meeting had been a divine appointment. I could not help but marvel at what an angel of mercy she had been.

As I turned to leave, Angel tossed her blond curls. "Best wishes to you!" she said joyfully, and was off. I never saw her again. "Was she an angel?" I wondered.

I left that place at ease. For several reasons, I knew this was not where I was called to be. I felt at peace. This was not a door I was supposed to walk through. I didn't know it then, but another door would open to me soon enough. It was one that would lead to more God adventures and some of the best and most fruitful years I had yet lived. A graduate college out East had accepted me! Additionally, they offered me a position where I could earn tuition remission working for them. I was stepping out into God's promises.

E.M. Bounds said in his book, *Answered Prayer*, "The only condition that restrains God's power and that disables Him to act is lack of faith. He is not limited in action nor restrained by the conditions that limit men."[2]

Surprising Encounters

Faith expects from God what is beyond all expectation.
—Andrew Murray

Our pastor shared a story that tremendously impacted my faith. It was the tale of Philip and his amazing transition from ministering to an Ethiopian on the side of the road to suddenly appearing in Azotus. If you study the geography, you will quickly see that Azotus is a substantial distance from Philip's point of origin.

According to Acts 8:5, Philip had been ministering to the city of Samaria, "proclaiming Christ to them."

> For in the case of many who had unclean spirits, they were coming out of them shouting with a loud voice; and many who had been paralyzed and lame were healed. So there was much rejoicing in the city.
>
> —Acts 8:7-8

God was doing mighty works! His good news was being preached throughout the region.

Then, as Phillip and the other apostles headed back to Jerusalem, Phillip was instructed to go to the southern road leading to Gaza. Philip's response was instant obedience. When he arrived there, he saw an Ethiopian eunuch, a court official for the Queen of Ethiopia, reading from the Book of Isaiah. At the Holy Spirit's prompting, Philip approached the eunuch asking him, "Do you understand what you are reading?" To which the eunuch replied, "Well, how could I, unless someone guides me?" (Acts 8:30-31). Immediately, Philip began explaining the Scripture and proclaiming Jesus.

In joy, the eunuch asked to be water baptized on the side of the road. This was followed by another amazing event. Philip disappeared! Scripture tells us that:

> When they came up out of the water, the Spirit of the Lord snatched Philip away; and the eunuch no longer saw him, but went on his way rejoicing. But Philip found himself at Azotus, and as he passed through he kept preaching the gospel to all the cities until he came to Caesarea.
>
> —Acts 8:39-40

Imagine being transported to another place to complete a new commission! This is precisely what happened to Philip who was merely being obedient. In reviewing our Bible, we find that such encounters are to be expected of God. According to the *New John Gill Exposition of the Whole Bible,* "The Spirit of the Lord took up Philip, just as he is said to lift up Ezekiel, between earth and heaven, and carried him above the earth as far as Azotus."[3] Ezekiel 8:3 conveys the vision given to him after being taken up.

> He stretched out the form of a hand and caught me by a lock of my head; and the Spirit lifted me up between earth and heaven and brought me in the visions of God to Jerusalem, to the entrance of the north gate of the inner court, where the seat of the idol of jealousy, which provokes to jealousy, was located.
>
> —Ezekiel 8:3

God always desires to show us things from His perspective, if we will only take the time to linger in His presence. In Philip's case, it was a physical transportation for another mission; he continued to preach the gospel to the cities from Azotus to Caesarea. In Ezekiel's case, it was to show him the abominations taking place in the temple and other things from a heavenly perspective. Both are miracles! But the best is yet to come as Jesus Himself said, "Truly, truly, I say to you, **he who believes in Me, the works that I do, he will do also; and greater works than these will he do; because I go to the Father**" (John 14:12).

Chapter 3

All Things Are Possible

With the Lord a day is like a thousand years, and a thousand years are like a day. The Lord is not slow in keeping his promise.

—2 Peter 3:8-9 NIV

MAKING ALL THINGS BEAUTIFUL

THE DAY HAD finally arrived! Israel stood on the brink of receiving its promise. God spoke to Moses directly as always saying that this was the land He was "going to give to the sons of Israel" (Numbers 13:2). This was meant to be the beginning of God's fulfillment of His covenant promise to Israel. God, who had parted the Red Sea on the Israelites' behalf and rescued them countless times before, would be with them. God, who was with them like a cloud by day and a pillar of fire by night, was leading them to their home (see Num. 9:15-23).

A leader from each of the twelve tribes of Israel was sent to spy out the land of Canaan. Thus, Moses sent the men out saying:

"Go up there into the Negev; then go up into the hill country. See what the land is like, and whether the people who live in it are strong or weak, whether they are few or many. How is the land in which they live, is it good or bad? And how are the cities in which they live, are they like open camps or with fortifications? How is the land, is it fat or lean? Are there trees in it or not? Make an effort then to get some of the fruit of the land." Now the time was the time of the first ripe grapes.

—Num. 13:17-20

Stuart Greaves says that receiving revelation from the Word of God is seeing a verse for the first time, although it existed before. It's as if God planted it when you were not looking, and when you see it, you see it for the first time.[4] In this verse, Moses was asking for fruit to be brought back to "encourage and animate the people in general, to go up and possess it (the land)."[5] According to *John Gill's Exposition of the Entire Bible,*

> *Now the time was the time of the first ripe grapes.*
> *Num. 13:17-20*

When they and the other summer fruits were coming to their perfection; and which was a proper season to see them in, and bring a sample of them; though Chaskuni suggests, that it was a more dangerous time to bring off fruit, because the keepers of the vineyards were then there; and hence they needed strengthening, and are bid to be of good courage... it must be about the middle of June; by which we may observe the forwardness of grapes in the land of Canaan, the time of vintage now drawing nigh.

It is interesting to me that at the same time *when the fruit was ready to be harvested, God's promises, too, were about to be fulfilled.* The fruit was ripe, nearing perfection. God ordered the time and season so that they would walk into His covenant promises at the perfect time.

The scripture from John 15 comes to mind as we discuss this. "I am the vine, you are the branches; he who abides in Me and I in him, he bears much fruit, for apart from Me you can do nothing" (John 15:5).

A FALSE REPORT

And yet, when the spies returned from scoping out the land, their report was mixed. Giants inhabited the land, they said. All, that is, except Joshua and Caleb. When Joshua and Caleb returned from spying out the land for Moses, they reported that the "land flows with milk and honey.... not fear the people of the land.... Their protection has been removed from them, and the Lord is with us" (Num. 14:8-10). Meanwhile, the others were afraid, for they said that, "All the people whom we saw in it are men of great size...and we became like grasshoppers in our own sight, and so we were in their sight" (Num. 13:32-33).

THE PROMISED LAND

According to *Matthew Henry's Commentary*, "Courage in such circumstances can only spring from strong faith, which Caleb and Joshua alone possessed" (Numbers 13:21-25).[6] Courage must spring from great faith. God had already been singing a love song over the Israelites in the wilderness. He had delivered them from Pharaoh and traveled with them day and night, giving them victory over their enemies. He had provided for them, nurtured them, and protected them. At last, the time had come to receive what God had promised them.

In spite of the obstacles ahead, God had promised them victory over their enemies. "He is exceedingly able to do...more than we could ask or think" (Eph. 3:20). Thus, we can choose to focus on those obstacles or the promise. Those who chose the promise, walked into it years later; those who did not, perished in the wilderness.

When we move forward believing in the promises He has clearly made, the unseen hand of God works in the background. We must simply say "yes" expecting that He is more than able to deliver us.

> Now was the time of the first ripe grapes.

PERFECT TIMING

For several years, I faithfully served our university, going to school while working a full-time job. I was an onstage actress at school while studying cinema, theatre, and divinity and working with incoming students. Although I felt so alive doing what I loved best, it was rigorous juggling my intense schedule.

Fortunately, my position working with the students paid for seventy-five percent of my tuition! (This was a side benefit of working for the school.) My position was helping incoming students adjust to the new and wonderful environment in which they would soon find themselves. It was my joy to interview students, help them along with their paperwork, and making recommendations to the faculty for acceptance. But after two years, I began to cry out. I dreamed of just being a student. I had helped so many others fulfill that dream. I just longed to live that life, albeit more simply. Oh, for the simplicity of enjoying my acting and communication classes, all the while learning more about Jesus!

Just before spring, I felt the Lord impress me to resign from my position at the school and apply for the President's Scholarship. Since only a few received this particular scholarship, and I was returning student, I could not help but wonder what my chances of getting it might be.

In addition, I felt awkward, since I knew the president and his wife personally. I had led intercession for the school with his wife, and they had seen me perform in plays on campus. So I thought, "I can't do that, Lord. I would feel as though I were taking advantage of their good nature." And yet, the Lord kept pressing me to submit the necessary paperwork.

In the meantime, He urged me to resign my position at the school. With no provision in sight, I hesitated. Yet, the wise words of Sylvia Evans, who had spoken at a women's conference just the year before, resonated in my ears. Sylvia had an incredible ministry as a healing and deliverance counselor through her church. She said, "I would not leave my position when the Lord first instructed me to do so. Then the anointing left, and I was forced to leave." Later, she went on to author numerous books, teach, counsel, and speak at conferences like the one I attended.

Meanwhile, a funny thing happened to me at work. The very month before I was supposed to resign, I found myself physically and emotionally fatigued from the workload. The mental duress and fear of struggling with when to quit my job plagued me. When I visited the doctor's office and explained my situation, the doctor looked at me calmly and said these words. "I think there is nothing wrong with you…that quitting your job won't fix." With that, she smiled, closed my folder, and left. I stared dumbfounded at her receding back. I felt validated that I was moving in the right direction.

As a final confirmation, one evening just before Easter, I "happened" to run into the president and his wife while exiting the theatre. With God knowing what was in my heart, I tentatively walked alongside them. After a fruitful conversation, the president's parting words to me were, "If there is anything we can do to help you, just let us know." This was indeed the exact confirmation I needed to proceed. The next day, I completed the application and submitted it. I will never forget the moment I slid it in the mail slot of the president's office that weekend. I wondered what was in store.

Just before I wrote my letter of resignation, I received a phone call from the president's office. "Could you come in for an interview?" the secretary asked. Excited, I responded with a calm, but fervent, "Yes!" Gazing at the sky while walking over to his office for my interview, I heard these words, "Go get your reward."

Although I was a strong candidate and highly favored, it would have to be God's will that I receive that scholarship. When I got to the president's office, and after a few questions, the president and I bowed our heads in prayer. As we closed our prayer, I heard a distinct voice say clearly, "Give it to her." It was profound. Hearing that voice was like hearing the Lord later say, "I call you Joy."

Simultaneously, the university's president and I raised our heads from prayer. His immediate words were, "I am giving this scholarship to you," he said quietly, "as an investment in the kingdom. Congratulations." He shook my hand and smiled, and I marveled as I turned to leave the office.

It was a blessing difficult to put into words. The Lord's hand had been upon me. The whole thing had been His doing. I finished out the remaining year and a half of my schooling as a full-time student. Although I was numb when I first received

In two weeks, I would be walking into His promises for me.

the news, I walked back to work and immediately put the finishing touches on my letter of resignation.

Upon graduation, I began my teaching career as a college professor. For several years since then, I have been privileged to be a part of many lives, watching the Lord work in the midst of them. Truly, I am grateful to the point of tears. Who knew that this journey would lead me down this path? All I can say is, "Thank You, Jesus!"

Worth More than Diamonds

"God's fingers can touch nothing but to mold it into loveliness."
—George MacDonald

O my dove, in the clefts of the rock,
In the secret place of the steep pathway,
Let me see your form,
Let me hear your voice;
For your voice is sweet,
And your form is lovely.

—Song of Solomon 2:14

HE KNOWS YOU BY NAME

THEY CALLED HER "Misfit." She was a tall, stocky teenager who some days waited outside my class for one of the young men in my class whom she was dating. Her beautiful green eyes were framed with dark make-up, and her short, jet-black hair was pulled up into two ponytails on the top of her head. She typically wore Gothic clothes and sported striped leggings to keep her warm in the brisk November air.

As I rounded the corner to class, I spied her sitting there. Arriving at class earlier than usual, I noticed that the class before mine had not yet let out. Smiling, I said "Hi. What's your name?" There was a pause. "Misfit," she replied looking down at her feet. "Oh," I said, somewhat surprised, but trying hard not to show it. "Hum. What name were you given at birth?" I asked gently. "Andrea," she softly replied.

"Andrea." I repeated, "That's a lovely name." She had only glanced up for that brief second. "Andrea," I said again gently, "where are you from?" And we began to talk. It turned out that she was originally from the Seattle area. Her family was very broken, so she had moved to Virginia at the age of fifteen seeking a new start. She was preparing to marry the young man in my class. He was twenty-one, and she was barely eighteen.

As we spoke, I watched her countenance soften. Each time I said, "Andrea," I could see a look of hope cross her face. I didn't know all she had been through, but this simple act of kindness softened her heart. It was obvious she had been rejected, told she didn't belong, and perhaps even that her conception had been an accident.

In those few precious moments we had together, I was able to sow in her heart the fact that she was a person made in God's image. She was a gem. We said our good-byes, and I stepped into class still feeling the sweet presence of the Lord. Turning just briefly, I smiled and said, "It was nice to meet you, Andrea." A small smile crossed her face. "It was nice to talk with you also."

REMEMBER

I am fearfully and wonderfully made.

—Ps. 139:14

> You are special. You are precious. You are not an accident. You were created with a purpose. [7]

Before He formed you in the womb, He knew you...He consecrated you. (Jeremiah 1:7). He blessed you with gifts. He chose you. Before the foundations of the earth, He predestined you. He knew you.

He sees you at your bedside, and He has stored up every tear you have ever cried. He knows your heart cry before you ever utter a prayer. He cares deeply about you. His desire is to comfort you. He has not forgotten you, nor will He. "Weeping may last for the night, but a shout of joy comes in the morning" (Ps. 30:5).

For Such a Time as This

> Call to Me and I will answer you, and I will tell you great and mighty
> things, which you do not know.
> —Jer. 33:3

She was a young maiden, an orphan until a family relative "took her as
his own daughter" (Esther 2:7). Unlike many orphan children today
who feel unloved or uncared for, this little girl was raised in a household
where she was cherished. Her uncle Mordecai taught her of their faith,
and she discovered a God who loved her dearly. In return, her heart
longed humbly to serve Him. Her uncle Mordecai continued to care for
her as his own until an appointed time. In the province in which they
lived, the day came for the king to choose a new queen.

Lovely in form and face, Esther caught the attention of the king's
attendants. They ushered her into the king's palace where she was given
beauty treatments in preparation for assuming the role of queen in the
event that the king chose her. Each day, Mordecai visited her to ensure
that she fared well. In wisdom, he instructed Esther not to reveal her
identity as a Jew, and so she was left to speak to God in secret (for the
times were perilous).

God gave Esther favor with all who saw her. A modest girl, she first
found favor with Hegai, chief overseer of all the aspiring young women.
He "quickly provided her with her cosmetics and food, gave her seven
choice maids from the king's palace and transferred her and her maids
to the best place in the harem" (Esther 2:9). After the twelve months of
beautification were completed, Esther finally met the king. According
to the story, the king "loved Esther more than all the women...so that
he set a royal crown on her head" (Esther 2:17).

God placed Esther in a pivotal role at a time in history when the
Jews were about to be persecuted. He put her in place *before* Haman,
an Agagite sworn to annihilate the Jews, ever rose to power. Thus, God
provided a deliverer for His beloved people before the need for one fully
manifested itself. When the news reached Mordecai of Haman's plot to
destroy the Jews, Esther's uncle and caregiver tore his clothes, wore ashes
and sackcloth, and wailed throughout the city. Esther sent her servant

Hathach to investigate the cause for Mordecai's weeping, only to learn of the edict that had been issued calling for the death of all Jews on the thirteenth day of the twelfth month.

Distraught, Esther knew not what to do, for she could not approach the king about such matters without being summoned by him. To enter the inner court of the king without his invitation meant death—even for a queen. Esther knew this, and replied to Mordecai. What could a woman like her do?

Mordecai replied with one of the most eloquent statements in history,

> Do not imagine that you in the king's palace can escape any more than all the Jews. For if you remain silent at this time, relief and deliverance will arise for the Jews from another place and you and your father's house will perish. And who knows whether you have not attained royalty for such a time as this?
>
> —Esther 4:13-14

Esther had been positioned by God and called to stand as an intercessor for her people. In Hebrew, the word used for intercession is *paga,* which means, "to meet."[8] Webster's dictionary defines the phrase "to intercede" in the following manner: "To go or pass between; to act between parties with a view to reconcile those who differ or contend; to mediate or make intercession." For further clarity, the same source distinguishes "to mediate" as "to interpose between parties as the equal friend of each; to mediate a peace; intercession."[9]

AT HIS FEET

In the words of C. Peter Wagner, "Prayer, generally speaking, means talking to God. Intercession is coming to God on behalf of another." After Mordecai's appeal to Esther regarding the plight of the Jews, Esther replied:

> Go, assemble all the Jews who are found in Susa, and fast for me; do not eat or drink for three days, night or day. I and my maidens also

will fast in the same way. And thus I will go in to the king, which is not according to the law; and if I perish, I perish.

—Esther 4:16

So, prior to this intervention, Esther not only set apart a period of prayer and fasting for herself, but also implored her people to pray on her behalf, likely for wisdom, favor, grace, and anointing. Strongholds were torn down so that when she presented herself, her plea might be heard and received.

According to C. Peter Wagner, "A special intimacy with God is high on the profile of intercessors. (In Esther's case) the king used his power to save the people of God."[10] Esther fulfilled her divine destiny by "going between" these two parties with a heart to see them reconciled. "As today's intercessors testify, the highest reward...is to be received in love by the Father and to see His power released for good through their intervention."[11]

Esther must have wondered if she would complete the task. She would need God's strength and wisdom. Once the great doors opened and she filed past the great royal court, she would need a miracle. To spare her life, the king needed to extend his golden scepter to her. Would he?

Indeed, he did! And he offered her half of the kingdom should she request it! Esther delayed her petition until she gave two banquets in honor of the king. There she revealed Haman's plot to destroy all the Jews, including her. Happily, the king revoked this murderous decree, established Mordecai as his right-hand man in place of Haman, and treasured Esther, his wife and queen.

Esther had humble beginnings, but God had marked her as His. He raised her up so that through her He might deliver the Jews. In a time of great distress, she fasted, prayed, and leaned on her Beloved. She became more than she could have imagined.

"For I know the plans I have for you," declares the LORD, "plans for welfare and not for calamity to give you a future and a hope."

—Jer. 29:11

CREATED FOR A PURPOSE

But my dove, my perfect one, is unique.

—Song of Solomon 6:9

For You formed my inward parts; You wove me in my mother's womb.

—Ps. 139:13

Your design is unique; there is no one like you.

—Song of Solomon 6:9

For everything created by God is good.

—1 Tim. 4:4

THE MIRACLE OF CREATION

In the beginning, one cell from your mom met one cell from your dad and you were formed! Do you realize what a miracle you are? According to Lou Giglio, an amazing process takes place in the womb as God fashions you together. It is indeed a holy process. At six months, one million neurotransmitters in your brain had to find the right one million transmitters in your eye. "One million seeking one million."[12] Now that's a miracle! Giglio goes on to say that, "When they all came together you had sight! But there was a fold of skin over your eye at the time. So mysteriously in the seventh month, a perfect cut was made in that skin to create your eyelid so that you could see."[13] The eye is still the most intricate and advanced technology on the planet! "The heavens are telling of the glory of God; and their expanse is declaring the work of His hands" (Ps. 19:1).

At the cellular level, microbiologists are discovering amazing things about the mechanisms inside each simple cell. Each cell contains enough DNA to build every kind of protein in your body![14] According to Michael Behe, a biochemist at Lehigh University, "a typical cell, which is a tenth of the size of the head of a pin, is composed of over three billion units of DNA."[15] Every piece of information was already present in the DNA code needed to fashion you. DNA functions like a software program;

more complex than anything anyone has ever devised. The genetic code for just one of these molecules would fill hundreds of pages of printed text. [16] Each of these cells is comprised of intricately arranged parts, a masterpiece of engineering and nanotechnology. [17] In the whole world, there is no one exactly like you! You are fearfully and wonderfully made! (Ps. 139:14).

And did you know that inside of your body is something called laminin? It may not sound spectacular, but laminin is a cell-adhesion molecule that holds your cells together. [18] It is also the "rebar" cell for the body. But here is the best part. This little cell is in the shape of a cross. Truly, you bear the signature of your Creator. [19] Jesus is literally holding you together.

> He is before all things, **and in Him all things hold together**.
> —Col. 1:17

Psalm 139:1-16 recounts that our form was not hidden from the Lord.

> For You formed my inward parts;
> You wove me in my mother's womb.
> I will give thanks to You, **for I am fearfully and wonderfully made;**
> Wonderful are Your works,
> And my soul knows it very well.
> **My frame was not hidden from You,**
> When I was made in secret,
> And **skillfully wrought** in the depths of the earth;
> Your eyes have seen my unformed substance;
> And in Your book were all written
> The days that were ordained for me,
> When as yet there was not one of them.

This adds new light to the passage from Jeremiah. "*Before* I formed you in the womb *I knew you,* and before you were born I consecrated you" (Jer. 1:5). I can imagine God smiling with joy imagining you as He put all your gifts and talents together, composed your hair and eye color, and chose the family and location He would place you in.

Interestingly enough, I have a friend named Guinevere, who had several prophetic dreams about her children before she ever conceived. In the dreams, her first child, a little girl, asked, "Mommie, when can I come out?" She looked at her future mother pleadingly. Puzzled, Guinevere awakened only to have the same dream again. Just before she was conceived, her little girl argued with Guinevere over what to name her. "I would like to name you Georgia." "Georgia," her little girl would say with disgust. "Absolutely not! My name is Tina." Indeed, that was the name she chose for her child. Tina means "follower of Christ."

> How precious also are Your thoughts to me, O God!
> How vast is the sum of them!
> If I should count them, they would outnumber the sand
> When I awake, I am still with You.
> —Ps. 139:17-18

Did you know that conservative estimates list 4×10^{21} grains of sand on the beaches of the earth![20] Yet imagine that *God's thoughts toward you even outnumber those grains of sand.* He is intimately acquainted with you—with your form and all that He made you to be.

> For we are His workmanship, created in Christ Jesus for good works, which God prepared beforehand so that we would walk in them.
> —Eph. 2:10

Arms Wide Open

He who goes to and fro weeping, carrying his bag of seed, shall indeed come again with a shout of **joy**, bringing his sheaves with him.

—Ps. 126:6

The answer to prayer is the part that glorifies God.

—E.M. Bounds

YOU ARE CHERISHED

SHE WAS A woman much beloved by her husband, Elkanah. He treasured her. Yet each year that passed brought no joyful news of a child. She was grieved in her heart and mocked by others for her childlessness. Penninah, Elkanah's other wife and her chief rival was jealous of Elkanah's love for Hannah and provoked her each time they met. As if she were not in enough pain, each time she heard the words, "childless" it was as if someone were rubbing salt deeper into her wound. Penninah's words were thoughtless and cruelly spoken.

Yet her husband loved her dearly, and did not resent her or the Lord. In seeing her earlier sadness, he said, "Hannah, why do you weep and why do you not eat and why is your heart sad? Am I not better to you than ten sons?" (1 Samuel 1:8) I imagine Elkanah lifting Hannah's chin gently with his finger so that their eyes met as he confessed his unshakable love for her. Troubled by Penninah's accusations, she might have had difficulty accepting this great gift. In a day and age when women sometimes based their identity on bearing children, the lack of them did not change her husband's feelings toward her.

Still, Hannah did not know why the Lord withheld His blessing for so long. On the day appointed for her to sacrifice, she went up to the house of the Lord with a soft heart. There at His feet, she poured out her complaint before the Lord. There she poured out her longings and her dreams. She laid them at His throne, much as David would years later in the Book of Psalms, when he said, "To Thee, O Lord, I call; My rock, do not be deaf to me…Hear the voice of my supplications when I cry to Thee for help" (Psalm 28:1a, 2). Like David's, Hannah's cry also ascended toward heaven.

> O Lord of hosts, if You will indeed look on the affliction of Your maidservant and remember me, and not forget Your maidservant, but will give Your maidservant a son, then I will give him to the Lord all the days of his life.
> —1 Sam. 1:11

And God heard her prayer. She was blessed by one of the priests and departed, no longer sad. When she returned to her husband, perhaps he noticed the change in her countenance; it was peaceful, expectant. God had heard her cry and promised her the desires of her heart. She left that place believing and expecting a miracle. She was ready to receive all that God had for her.

That very night, the Lord remembered her. As she and her husband came together, a child was knit together in her womb. This child would be a blessing to many and a leader in the House of Israel. He would help restore rightful worship before the Lord, anoint and guide the first kings of Israel, and speak prophetic words over the nation. God had indeed remembered Hannah and given her the desires of her heart. He was looking for a willing vessel, and He found one in her.

E.M. Bounds once said in his book, *Answered Prayer*, that:

> It is not abject prostration of the body before God, or the exquisite beauty and poetry of the diction of our prayers that do the deed, act or

attitude. It is not the marvelous array of eloquence in praying that makes prayer effectual…**It is the answer that brings glory to God.**[21]

James 4:2-3 states, "You do not have because you do not ask. You ask and do not receive because you ask with wrong motives, so that you may spend it on your pleasures."

Hannah gave Samuel to the Lord all the days of his life, but the story does not end there. Scripture goes on to tell us that Hannah had three more sons and two daughters. And each year Hannah and her husband visited the house of the Lord, bringing a priestly robe for her little boy, a reminder of God's faithfulness.

> For by these He has granted to us His precious and magnificent promises.
>
> —2 Peter 1:4

ANSWERED PRAYER

One of my dear friends, Abigail, recently married and settled in to begin this new phase of her life. She was an avid performer, appearing in local theatre and film roles, which gained her much acclaim. Critics lauded her as one of the most talented actresses in the area, particularly for her singing ability. But her most poignant performance was about to be given.

She and I were cast in an encore performance of a play we had performed in graduate school. Although this production featured various women from the Bible, Abigail's performance as Sarah touched me the most. Only the close-knit cast and crew knew that she and her husband had been trying for more than a year for a child. As Abigail sang and spoke of Sarah's longing for a child, I teared up backstage. We all offered up special prayers that God would hear and touch her.

When I saw Abigail three months later, something seemed different. Later, she confided that she had become pregnant on the very eve of the performance! God had

> The very hairs upon your head are numbered.
>
> *Matt 10:30*

seen and heard her cry, and had given her the desire of her heart. Today, they have a beautiful baby boy, and the knowledge that when we ask God for bread; He will never give us a stone. (Matt. 7:9)

A CLOSE CALL

"He is watching over His Word to perform it."

God's love and tender mercies amaze me. Each one of us is precious in His sight, and He longs to enfold us in His embrace. Someone who understands that well is a former student of mine, Mindy. I will never forget the day she approached me about giving a speech on the topic of abortion. Although we debate it each semester to educate students on the dangers and ethics of abortion, I needed a reprieve. It was a popular topic, but so gut-wrenching that I had taken it off the list that semester.

Curious, I asked, "Why would you like to debate it?" Mindy smiled. "I have a story to tell you, Professor Joy." And so she began. Years ago, her mother had become pregnant out of wedlock and had considered an abortion. Without her parents' knowledge, she made an appointment and arrived at the clinic with that intention. The nurse had shown her in. She had filled out the appropriate paperwork and had gotten Mindy's mother strapped onto the table.

It was at that moment that Mindy's mother had second thoughts. She began to get off the table, but was discouraged from doing so by the doctor. Finally, she broke free from his grip, and made her way out of the clinic. "Professor Joy," Mindy paused, "I was the child my mother was carrying." Her eyes met mine. "If she had not left there, you would never have met me," said the blonde-haired, blue-eyed young woman standing before me. As I brushed a tear from my eyes, I said quietly, "You can do that speech."

Mindy was passionate about her topic. She wanted to hammer it into the class that abortion was wrong by showing graphic photos, describing the process of abortion, and discussing the deep depression most mothers experience afterwards. As passionate as she was, I could see that she was not conveying God's love for women who had been through this situation. Someone once said, "They'll never care about what you know unless they know that you care."

It was no accident that Mindy had been placed in this class. We prayed together, seeking God's face in the matter and asking that someone in the class would be touched. "I just keep getting this impression that there's someone in this class who needs to hear this," I said. God impressed it upon our hearts that, "She is making a decision between life and death. And this speech could speak life and truth to her." Having listened to God's heartbeat, the way Mindy composed the speech took a dramatic turn. Instead of focusing on the graphic images of aborted babies, Mindy decided to begin with her story.

Mindy prepared and practiced until finally the day for her speech arrived. She was the first to speak that day and the last. Smiling at the class, she began to share her story. At first, the class was put off by the topic. Some were even offended at her stance, until she began to share her mother's story.

You could hear a pin drop when she finished. I watched as hearts were softened. People cried and listened intently as she shared with love the truth about abortion. I was so proud of her.

After class, Claudia, another student, approached Mindy. (Claudia had given a speech previously entitled "Why Girls Should Have a Pet to Care for Before Even Thinking about Having a Baby.") She solemnly approached Mindy and said simply, "A close friend of mine is pregnant, and I was encouraging her to have an abortion." She paused, her eyes meeting Mindy's, "I am going to share with her what you spoke about today." She added, "I don't believe any more that she should have an abortion, and I am going to stand with her. She is carrying a child."

I have seen other girls touched by the discovery of life beginning in the womb. It astonishes me how God's truth sets the captive free. Such was the story of Claudia and later, Sarah.

PLANTING SEEDS

For as the rain and the snow come down from heaven, and do not return there without watering the earth and making it bear and sprout, and furnishing seed to the sower and bread to the eater; so will My word be which goes forth from My mouth; it will not return to Me empty, without accomplishing what I desire, and without succeeding in the matter for which I sent it.

—Isa. 55: 10-11

As stated earlier, each semester, students choose a debate topic that most interests them. Then they break into groups of five and debate both sides of the issue. Two choose one side to explore, two choose the other and one person mediates. As one of the debate groups prepared to present, Sarah shyly approached me. She had been researching the pro-choice side of the abortion argument. "There's something I would like to share with you after class," she said, smiling. "All right," I replied, curious.

Sarah was a tall, athletic young lady who had been outspoken on her topic. Although she presented the pro-choice side well, she informed the class at the end of her speech that she was now pro-life. She had changed her mind.

I smiled, encouraged. There was more. As the rest of the students filed out of the classroom, I noticed Sarah waiting for me. She approached me slowly as if she had a precious secret to tell. "I wanted to let you know, Professor Joy," she confided, "that I just found out I am pregnant and I would like to keep my baby." Sarah continued on, "Doing all this research for the side I was on, looking at the pictures of these children..." she paused, "I just wanted you to know."

> God is always working—whether we see it or not.

I began to tear up. We hugged and I thanked God.

Indeed, the very hairs of your head are all numbered. Do not fear; you are more valuable than many sparrows.

—Luke 12:7

Chapter 6

Romanced

You will be a crown of beauty in the hand of the Lord.

—Isa. 62:3

YOU ARE LOVED

SHE WAS A woman from a foreign land, a gentle and demure young widow. Robed in simple clothes, she made a perilous journey into a new land; yet it was one of destiny. There, someone would behold her surrendered and beautiful heart in the midst of difficult circumstances. For it is, "the hidden person of the heart, with the imperishable quality of a gentle and quiet spirit, which is precious in the sight of God" (1 Peter 3:4).

In the land of Moab, Ruth and her sister-in-law had lost their husbands tragically. The men had been the only sons of Naomi, an ailing widow. When it came time for her mother-in-law to depart for Bethlehem, Ruth clung to her. In a moment of truth, she expressed her loyalty. "Do not urge me to leave you or turn back from following you; for where you go, I will go, and where you lodge, I will lodge. Your people shall be my people, and your God, my God" (Ruth 1:16). Ruth's sincerity touched her mother-in-law's heart, and the two were off to Bethlehem, which means "house of bread."

Not only was Ruth committed to making the journey with her mother-in-law; she became a faithful companion and friend to Naomi. God's plan for them was not finished yet. In spite of their losses, He was weaving a beautiful tapestry of redemption in both their lives. For Ruth, it would be a new love, and for Naomi, a hope and a future.

A Love Story

Ruth was gleaning in a field where the Lord had led her. Her mother-in-law had learned of a near kinsman who might have grain in abundance, and so Ruth said, "Please let me go to the field and glean among the ears of grain after one in whose sight I may find favor" (Ruth 2:2).

As she gleaned, the Lord indeed gave her favor. She was at the right place at the right time. Boaz, Naomi's near kinsman, noticed and inquired after her. Upon hearing of her sacrifice, and the good she had done for her mother-in-law, he spoke gently to her, encouraging and protecting her:

> All that you have done for your mother-in-law after the death of your husband has been fully reported to me, and how you left your father and your mother and the land of your birth, and came to a people that you did not previously know. May the Lord reward your work, and your wages be full from the Lord, the God of Israel, under whose wings you have come to seek refuge.
>
> —Ruth 2:11-12

And so Boaz cared for, provided for, and blessed Ruth. Boaz even commanded his servants to "drop" some extra grain in her path while they were harvesting to make it easier for her to gather plenty. He also protected her by ordering none of his servants to touch her as she gathered grain with the other maids. He encouraged her to draw water if she was thirsty, and to eat with the reapers. He even served her roasted grain himself.

When Ruth returned home with the news, Naomi was ecstatic. There was more to come. Upon learning of Boaz's identity, a thunderstruck Naomi saw God's potential plan for them. It was customary in those days for a kinsman redeemer to rise up and aid a widow who was his closest family. This near kinsman could marry a widow and care for her family. Naomi therefore instructed her daughter-in-law in this way with regard to Boaz:

> Wash yourself therefore, and anoint yourself and put on your best clothes, and go down to the threshing floor…It shall be when he lies down, that you shall notice the place where he lies, and you shall go and uncover his feet and lie down; then he will tell you what you shall do.
>
> —Ruth 3:3-4

Thus, when Boaz awoke and discovered a woman at his feet, he inquired who she was. Ruth said simply, "I am Ruth your maid. So spread your covering over your maid, for you are a close relative" (Ruth 3:9).

Now envision Boaz's surprise and delight, for before him knelt a virtuous woman making an honorable request. Imagine that all of this time during the barley and wheat harvest, Boaz had been able to observe Ruth, her modesty, her commitment to honor her mother-in-law, and her desire to learn the ways of God. Boaz called her "a woman of excellence," for this was how she was known in the city (Ruth 3:11).

Ruth was obedient to leave her family and all that was familiar by stepping out in faith, and God had blessed her. He had met her where she needed it most. Scripture tells us that Ruth kept her heart pure by not going after younger men and marrying. She waited and was placed at the heart of one of the most beautiful love stories yet written. She was placed in the harvest field of Boaz, her future husband. She would bear a child, Obed.

But the story does not end there; for Ruth is written into a lineage she could not have imagined…that of Jesus.[22] "So they named him Obed. He is the father of Jesse, the father of David" (Ruth 4:17). Ruth is later mentioned in the Book of Matthew where "the genealogy of Jesus the Messiah, the son of David, the son of Abraham" is recorded (Matt. 1:1). "Boaz was the father of Obed by Ruth" (Matt. 1:5).

God wrote a love story for Ruth and Boaz, and gave Naomi the gift of hope in old age as she watched her little grandson grow. She, too, was now under Boaz' protection all the days of her life. As her friends echoed:

> Blessed is the Lord who has not left you without a redeemer today, and may his name become famous in Israel. May he also be to you a restorer of life and a sustainer of your old age; for your daughter-in-law, who loves you and is better to you than seven sons, has given birth to him.
>
> —Ruth 4:14-15

God writes exquisite love stories. His love for us is beyond what we can imagine at times. He truly does make all things beautiful just in time (see Eccl. 3:11).

> Behold, I will do something new, now it will spring forth; will you not be aware of it? I will even make a roadway in the wilderness, rivers in the desert. Because I have given waters in the wilderness and rivers in the desert, to give drink to My chosen people.
> The people whom I formed for Myself will declare My praise.
>
> —Isa. 43:19-21

EXTRAVAGANT LOVE

Some of my favorite stories are God-stories such as Ruth's where God sees our hearts, knows our struggles, and gives us grace to be faithful in the dry seasons. During each period of sowing and reaping, He lavishes His love upon us. He is our source, our strength, and our provider. We have already received the greatest gift of all, His Son, making all other gifts just additional expressions of His extravagant love for us. If it is His desire to give and entrust these things to us, we should receive them with joy. Trust that He has the best in store.

Take heart, beloved, the Lord has a plan for you.

Who better to craft our love stories than the One who knows and loves us best? He is the One with whom we share our secrets as well as our triumphs. Since He is intimately acquainted with us, who better to choose our mate? And, in the meantime, He gives us a delicious season where He has us all to Himself!

God overwhelmed me once with a dream trip to England. I had often traveled to second and third world countries to help whenever I could during my vacation time. This summer would be different, and from it, I would learn some incredible lessons of God's love for me.

Every good thing given and every perfect gift is from above.
                                                          —James 1:17

It was August. The weather outside was wonderful, and I was in England! As I woke and rose from my cozy bed, I pulled back the sheers and peeked out the balcony window. There before me the streets of London unfolded. Pristine, white townhouses, green lawns, and enclosed parks dotted my view.

"I am in London!" I sighed as I fell back onto the soft, queen-sized bed. One more dream had come true. This trip was God's gift to me after finishing my coursework in graduate school while teaching. Curling up under the covers and closing my eyes, I scrunched my nose and asked, "So, what are we doing today, Lord?"

My days in London were dreams come true. They were filled with unexpected surprises and always the knowledge that the Creator, God, was taking good care of me. I felt overwhelmed with gratitude and love—as if my heart were singing in my chest. He truly was watching over me.

I got up and began to prepare for whatever lay ahead. Going down to breakfast, I was greeted by delightful, smiling cooks who had seen me coming and prepared my favorite fresh scrambled eggs and toast with real jam. I pinched myself. These people were strangers when I first arrived. Now an older woman with a thick Turkish accent said, winking, "We made these especially for you."

I settled in to read my Bible, catch the brilliant British news, and sip my tea. It had been a lovely trip so far: a journey to Brighton Beach, Hampton Court, and my favorite...the white cliffs of Dover. How did one take it all in? Content and refreshed by the meal, I scampered off to gather my things. "What is in store?" I wondered excitedly.

On the way to the Tube, about two blocks down the street, was one of my favorite delicatessens. I can still taste the pastries—wonderfully fluffy rolls filled with fruit and real Devonshire cream. It was a piece of heaven! Being mindful of the heat, however, I passed up the pastries, and got a lovely cheese and vegetable sandwich with a cookie. I headed for the Tube. The weather looked a bit foreboding now, but one never knew in London. *Always prepare for rain*, I thought as I hustled to my stop.

No more heavy coins to carry or waiting in long lines. I now owned a pass that would allow me to ride anywhere all day with the swipe a card. Smiling gleefully as I swept past newcomers to London, I sighed contentedly. *I looked lost like that once a few weeks ago,* I reflected, seeing a young man in a trench coat asking for directions. A kindhearted bobbie—policeman—assisted him.

In the distance, I heard the delicious sound of music echoing through the corridors as I descended the escalator into the Tube. It was as if I had accidentally happened upon a concert. As I descended on the escalator, I spied a young Korean man playing the violin very expressively. Those delightful notes ascended into the heavens as he seemed to worship with his eyes closed. I marveled, reached into my pocket, and tossed some money into his hat.

Arriving at my station, I saw a flurry of activity. It was raining heavily now. But, having spent a week or so in Ireland on my way to England, I was accustomed to getting soaked. I zipped up my raincoat and to the tune of "Singing in the Rain," began the long walk to "The Proms." Since it had been one of my father's dreams to attend a concert at Royal Albert Hall, I was going in part to photograph the event, hoping that it might inspire him to make the trip. For those of you who may be wondering what "the Proms" are, let me enlighten you.

Every summer, a series of concerts is held all over England in locations like Hyde Park, Castle Howard, and of course, my destination, Royal Albert Hall. In order to attend the famed "Last Night of the Proms," your name must be drawn from a lottery. Watching it on television with my father, I had to admit I had never seen anything quite like it. Hundreds of audience members in colorful, patriotic costumes dance in time with the music and interact with a live orchestra. It is a grand affair.

Royal Albert Hall was built by Queen Victoria to honor her late husband, Prince Albert. I gathered from all of the portraits and statues I saw of them, the two had been greatly in love. They had had five beautiful children together, and his untimely death caused her great sorrow.

In order to raise funds to build the Hall, Queen Victoria offered patrons the option to purchase lifetime seats to attend every concert held there. For the mere price of three hundred pounds, a seat could then be passed down to succeeding generations.

By the time I reached the Hall, it was literally pouring. Trying to stay somewhat dry, I made my way around its great exterior only to be thwarted from entering. However, on my way back around the loop, I happened upon a couple from South America. "Are you here for the free concert too?" the husband asked holding his umbrella up to shelter his wife from the downpour. "Free concert?" I replied, stunned. He smiled, "Follow us," and led me to an open door.

Once inside, I brushed off, grabbed my lunch, and settled in to listen to a stringed quartet. I could hardly believe my luck! Here I was inside Royal Albert Hall (well, I was in the elaborately decorated restaurant located just inside its walls) listening to a free concert. Happily, I ate my sandwich in peace. *So this is what we are doing today*, I said (or rather thought), smiling. But there was more.

After the concert, I took a breathtaking tour of the hall itself, learning much of its history. Then, arriving at the top rim of the hall, I heard the most beautiful sound. It was as if angels were singing. Some of the musicians were rehearsing a piece far below. As their notes floated up to the heavens, I wiped away a tear. "I wish my father could hear this," I sighed. It was some of the most exquisite music I had ever heard.

Later that week, I attended a concert in the Hall itself. Although this popular performance was almost sold out, my ticket had been surprisingly easy to come by. I chose a seat close to the orchestra so that I could see the musicians' faces more clearly. As I entered the Hall, I tried to take in all of its three levels. The Hall had been completely redone just a few years earlier. Red velvet seat cushions, curtains, and gold trim added to its majestic look.

As I settled in, a distinguished-looking couple in their sixties took their seats beside me. They were a friendly couple with an aristocratic air about them. *Am I sitting next to royalty?* I wondered. Although the wife was casually attired, her husband wore a dignified black suit and sported an ivory-handled walking cane. We chatted about it a bit.

It turned out that they were the happy recipients of some of those famous tickets, purchased during Queen Victoria's era. Although I never got a true confession of their birthright, they exuded kindness mingled with decorum. "So this is what royalty is like," I murmured.

It taught me a lesson I will never forget. True royalty knows its position, and yet there was no pride associated with it. Instead, I found a profound sense of dignity coupled with humility, or power under restraint. Their kindness and genuine concern for me was mingled with a deep sense of knowing who they were.

We are royalty. We are children of the King. The Father loves us, and we are His.

> But you are a chosen race, a royal priesthood, a holy nation, a people for God's own possession, so that you may proclaim the excellencies of Him who has called you out of darkness into His marvelous light.
> —1 Peter 2:9

A MAGICAL MANOR

Ashburnham Place is a magical manor in the south of England, complete with walking trails, bridges, and lakes filled with water lilies. Formerly a manor, it had been converted into a retreat center for churches and individuals by its new owner, a minister. I was fortunate enough to spend three days there: walking the grounds, feasting with new friends, and spending precious time with the Lord.

As I made my way to the dining hall, I was surprised to find one lone table fully decorated and awaiting me. It had a sage green curtain for privacy and all the amenities I had experienced with a group the evening prior. Puzzled, I returned to the front desk and asked, "Excuse me. Where will I be sitting tonight?"

The previous evening, I had met new friends who were also spending a time of retreat at Ashburnham. The waiter had seated all of us together as guests and served us a delightful meal using a real silver service. But tonight was different.

"Follow me, please," the lady politely said as she led me right back to that table. "Here?" I replied. "Well, yes," she said smiling, "there are no other guests. We figured since you were on retreat, you might like to have the whole place to yourself."

I was profoundly moved. "All for me?" I queried. Although I could see a church group in another room, this room had been set aside for me. "Yes," she replied kindly. "They will serve everything they normally serve, just like last night, but tonight it is all for you." With that, she cheerfully twirled around to return to her station, saying, "The waiter will be with you shortly."

I sat down, unfolded the napkin, and placed it in my lap. On the table, draped with a white linen tablecloth, sat a lovely basket of fruit. Beside it were two candlesticks and all the amenities a traditional dinner entails. I marveled as a young waiter in a coat and tails entered, pushing a silver cart with various trays. "What would you like, madam?" he asked. He served me and then he left me to ponder this gift.

I marveled and a tear rolled down my cheek. It was not about numbers. The King of kings and the Lord of lords had prepared a feast just for me.

> He has brought me to his banquet hall, and **his banner over me is love.**
>
> —Song of Solomon 2:4

Waiting on God

The Lord is my shepherd, I shall not want. He makes me lie down in green pastures; He leads me beside quiet waters. He restores my soul.

—Ps. 23:1-3

Surely goodness and mercy shall follow me
All the days of my life they follow me
Surely I'm going to dwell in the House of the Lord
Forever and ever and ever and ever more.

—Jason Upton's *Psalm 23*

DIVINE APPOINTMENTS

IT WAS MY last day in London. (Sigh.) The trip so far had been a marvelous one. As I got ready to set off for the rugged green of Scotland in the morning, I pondered how to spend my last afternoon in this delightful city. Among my favorite places to walk were the greens and parks of Holland Park and Kensington. There, lavish English gardens awaited me along with lanes of beautiful, turn-of-the-century homes.

But I was alone. And today I felt it. Sitting mournfully on a bench underneath the canopy of shade trees, I made my plight known to God. Back then thoughts of a recent break-up with a young man were still fresh in my head. My thoughts were not very positive as I gazed at the symphony of rare flowers surrounding me.

Without warning, I spied a lady making her way through the garden by way of an elaborate cobblestone path. "She's wearing a hat much like mine," I mused. It was a colorful sunhat crumpled from a bit of traveling. I watched as she gazed at each of the unoccupied benches before settling on mine. "How do you do?" she introduced herself with a slight Scandinavian accent. What was God up to? Somehow, I sensed this was a divine appointment. "I am well," I politely replied. And so our afternoon began.

She was a teacher, I discovered over lunch at one of the cafes only locals know about. She shared several stories from her country before we discovered that we were both Christian ladies traveling on holiday alone. To top it all off, as we walked through some of my favorite haunts in Holland Park, she mentioned that she was in a dilemma and had been praying for someone to talk with about it. In fact, she had been struggling to mention it throughout our conversations.

"I saw you sitting there with that hat on and I thought, 'She looks friendly.' I felt the Holy Spirit draw me." She said she was having difficulty in her relationship with her boyfriend.

I smiled. The warm sun winked down at us through the trees as we strolled past the white town homes of Holland Park, one of the areas where I had longed to travel. "What seems to be the trouble?" I queried. She sighed and began to unfold her story. She had been married before, but had remained good friends with her ex-husband. They both still lived in the same town! Recently, she had begun dating a new man. "He is not as attentive," she said. "I feel as though I am doing most of the work in the relationship." She gave several scenarios. One example was when he had promised to call and then had forgotten.

At that time, I knew almost exactly how she felt. "This is no coincidence that we met today," I said softly. "I was also praying for someone to talk to. And here we are." Together, we spent a delightful day in some of my favorite spots as God poured into us. I will never forget taking the Tube back with her as the day came to an end. We traveled the same route together, but my stop was just before hers. As the Tube neared the station, I saw the realization hit her. "Thank you," she said slowly. "This has been a divine appointment."

As the train arrived at its station and we said our good-byes, I hopped off onto the platform. I looked up to the heavens and said smiling, "Another perfect day. Today, You were my comforter."

> Now on the last day, the great day of the feast, Jesus stood and cried out, saying, "If anyone is thirsty, let him come to Me and drink. He who believes in Me, as the Scripture said, 'From his innermost being will flow rivers of living water.'"
>
> —John 7:37-38

HE IS YOUR COMFORTER

Many times in my young adult life, I faced the challenging stares of others who wondered how I remained single for so long. At first, the choice to wait for God's best was heralded as a wise and worthy sacrifice. Then, when I entered into my late twenties without the prospect of marriage, I met stares of surprise and hurtful whispers. People who had known me for years suddenly began to give me looks of pity. I tried to remain steadfast. There were times I wept openly before the Lord, as David had done when pondering his fate in the Caves of Adullah. "Had I missed it?" I pondered. "Is there something I could do?" I was confident that God loved me, and that others found me desirable.

Each sling and dagger thrown scraped at my shield of faith. It was a battle, but one must battle doubt with *faith*. Someone once said, "Do not doubt in the dark what God spoke in the light." In fact, *The Fire of Delayed Answers* by Bob Sorge ministered deeply to my spirit in that season. In the book, Sorge discusses God's timing in preparing His people to receive the promises of God. Joseph, David, Job, and others are mentioned with these parallels drawn. Here, the story of Sarah comes to mind as we examine God's loving kindness and faithfulness despite Sarah's failings (and her attempts to interfere with God's plans and promises).

Reading *Lady in Waiting* by Kendall and Jones also encouraged me greatly. Several sections that spoke truth to me included being a lady of security and conviction. They wrote, "Why do women feel they must go after men? Many women have believed a lie. They think, 'I must get the best for myself because God may not give it to me.'"[23] Deeply convicted, I realized that I had not trusted God to bring His best to me.

I had chased men I was interested in for as long as I could remember! In desperation, I considered men who had great potential if only they changed! I needed to surrender the whole thing to God.

Imagine God's excitement for a gift He has prepared for you to open. It is Christmas and He has a special gift set aside with a lovely red and white bow waiting to be unwrapped. You cannot wait to pop the top off as He watches your expression of sheer delight and surprise. In the meantime, remember if you are waiting, that you are a woman of faith, who is deeply loved by God. You are only waiting for God's heart to be revealed…trusting that God has the best yet in store.

When I finally surrendered the matter to the Lord, I had peace. For the first time in my life, there was no reason to strive. I simply needed to receive God's best for me. My loving Father indeed had the perfect person picked out for me.

MOTHER OF A NATION

She was the beloved wife of the father of a nation. In her earlier years, God had promised Abram, her husband, a son, and that Abram would have as many descendents as there are stars in the sky.

> And He [God] took him outside and said, "Now look toward the heavens, and count the stars, if you are able to count them." And He said to him, "So shall your descendents be." Then he believed the Lord; and He reckoned it to him as righteousness.
>
> —Gen. 15:5-6

What a vision! God takes you outside, puts His arm around your shoulder, and points to the stars in the heavens. What a promise from a personal God!

What most people often forget about is how long Abram and Sarai waited until God's word was fulfilled. Sadly, Sarai reached a point where she lost hope, for she took Hagar, her Egyptian maid, to Abram to conceive on Sarai's behalf. She acted in her own strength, rather than believing the Word of the Lord spoken to her husband. And out of that union came Ishmael.

Yet, God redeemed Sarai's mistake; He had mercy on her. Most importantly, God made an incredible covenant with Abram and Sarai that He was faithful to fulfill, changing their names to Abraham and Sarah in the process. (But that is another story!)

> As for Sarai your wife, you shall not call her name Sarai, but Sarah shall be her name. I will bless her, and indeed I will give you a son by her. Then I will bless her, and she shall be a mother of nations; kings of peoples will come from her.
>
> —Gen. 17:15-16

Upon hearing this, Abraham laughed, imagining having a son at one hundred with a wife of ninety years of age! Yet God was firm. He would bless Ishmael as Abraham asked, but it would be through Isaac that His marvelous promises and covenant would remain. In Genesis 18:10, we read God's promises about to be fulfilled. For God sent three messengers ahead, and this time it was Sarah herself who heard the promise, "I will surely return to you at this time next year; and behold, Sarah your wife will have a son." And Sarah laughed. Yet came the reply from one of them, "Is anything too difficult for the Lord?" (Gen. 18:14).

Sarah was in her later years when Isaac was born. Although he arrived much later in life than Sarah had planned, the important thing to remember is that: *he was born.* The birth pangs and work God did in her heart were both purposeful and fruitful. In the Book of Hebrews we learn that:

> Faith is the assurance of things hoped for, the conviction of things not seen. For by it the men of old gained approval. And without faith it is impossible to please Him, for he who comes to God must believe that He is and that He is a rewarder of those who seek Him.
>
> —Heb. 11:1-2, 6

One of the greatest indictments against the people of Israel was their lack of faith. It was their unbelief that kept them out of the Promised Land and wandering in the wilderness for many years.

And yet, it pleases God greatly when we believe His Word and what He has spoken to our hearts. *It pleases Him.* By believing in Him, it demonstrates our trust in Him—our willingness to follow where He leads. His heart is moved. I imagine that, like a doting Father, He smiles in contentment as we eagerly take hold of His hand in surrender, and go with Him on the journey. He desires the best for us because He loves us. And even if, like Sarah, we make missteps along the way, He can redeem those mistakes, forgiving us.

BUILDING A BOAT

Perhaps my favorite story of faith comes from the Book of Genesis. "By faith Noah, being warned by God about things not yet seen, in reverence prepared an ark for the salvation of his household" (Heb. 11:7).

Now if you investigate the story of Noah, you'll discover a few things. One, it took him 120 years to build the ark with his three sons. Two, there was no such thing as rain back then, since the dew watered the earth.[24]

I can imagine some of Noah's friends visiting him on site and scratching their heads. "Hey, Noah, what are you building?" they ask mockingly.

"An ark," Noah patiently replies.

Someone else asks, "What's an ark?"

Noah then gestures to the structure behind him, while sipping on some refreshment.

Still confused they jeer. "But what's it for?"

Patiently Noah explains, "God commanded me to build an ark. He said there's going to be a flood."

"A flood!" they smirk. Laughter erupts.

I can imagine Noah shaking his head in sadness as he looks at them and then looks to the heavens for peace before beginning his work again. It took a lot of faith to build that ark. One hundred twenty years with some painful persecution, to be sure.

To read a litany of praises about God's faithful people, please review Hebrews 11.

> But it was what God had spoken to Noah, and so he persevered.

By faith Abraham, when he was called, obeyed by going out to a place, which he was to receive for an inheritance; and he went out, not knowing where he was going.

By faith he lived as an alien in the land of promise, as in a foreign land, dwelling in tents with Isaac and Jacob, fellow heirs of the same promise; **For he was looking for the city, which has foundations, whose architect and builder is God.**

By faith even Sarah herself received ability to conceive, even beyond the proper time of life, since she considered Him faithful who had promised.

Therefore there was born even of one man, and him as good as dead at that, as many descendants **as the stars of heaven in number, and innumerable as the sand, which is by the seashore**.

—Heb. 11:8-12

Faith truly is the assurance of things hoped for. And God, who sees everything, gazes at the tapestry and sees it as it will be when it is finished. Standing back, He smiles at the beautiful artwork He has created. Remember, "It is the answer to prayer that glorifies God."[25]

Blessed be the God and Father of our Lord Jesus Christ, the Father of mercies and God of all comfort, **who comforts us in all our affliction so that we will be able to comfort those who are in any affliction with the comfort with which we ourselves are comforted by God.** For just as the sufferings of Christ are ours in abundance, so also our comfort is abundant through Christ.

—2 Cor. 1:3-5

I will never forget sitting down to lunch with a former student. She was lamenting her sudden singleness when these encouraging words sprung from my mouth. "What if God just wanted you all to Himself for a little while?" I smiled.

> No time spent with God is ever wasted.

She lifted her head, eyes wide in revelation. "Yes," she repeated now with a smile slowly spreading across her face, "what if He did?"

You are valuable. He cherishes the time He spends with you.

Chapter 8

You Are Beautiful

You are altogether beautiful, my darling, and there is no blemish in you.

—Song of Solomon 4:7

SET FREE

DRIVING MY CAR one night, I happened upon a radio show that caught my attention. To this day, I do not recall the speaker's name, but I shall never forget his message. He was speaking on the subject of purity while sharing a true story of something that had happened to Shana, a young woman at a local summer camp.

Shana was thirteen years old that summer. A girl who had suffered molestation at an early age, by the time she was eleven she had begun seeking comfort in the arms of boys. She was a beautiful young girl with green, almond-shaped eyes; Shana had the winsome quality of one who has seen much, but still maintained a childlike innocence.

Travis, one of the camp counselors, was heartbroken when he heard of her situation. Each day he watched as she shyly flirted with some of the young boys. Her eyes sparkled as they expressed interest and stole glances at her young form. She moved gracefully, revealing her newly found curves with clothes that were sexy, but not indecent. Each feigned look of surprise or smile as she pretended to listen to their bravado drew the young men closer. Subtly, Shana lured her camp mates. Yet as Travis noted, Shana seemed to care more about what they thought about her, than she cared personally for them. Under all of her actions was a cry for approval and acceptance.

Later, as he watched her gaze off into the distance while leaning on a tree, it seemed to him that Shana was in a world of her own. Her eyes looked longingly at the landscape that stretched for miles to the horizon. She appeared to be saddened after her performance. Deep within her, Travis guessed, there was a profound insecurity in her value or beauty.

During the last few evenings of camp, a series of prayer meetings were held. All of the campers were invited to attend, and indeed Shana was there in her corner flirting with her posse and laughing in a way that made her seem even more beautiful. Travis prayed that somehow the messages that had been shared about her value before God would reach her.

After the last meeting, Travis ran across Shana outside. Her long hair was blowing freely in the wind and the moon painted her silhouette against the night sky. He could see she had been crying, but there was nothing sad about her countenance. "Shana?" he gently asked.

Shana swept away a tear from her eye. Slowly, she smiled and lifted her gaze to meet his. She had listened to the message and surrendered her heart to Christ earlier that evening.

"Are you all right?" Travis tentatively asked.

Shana took another peaceful breath before replying. "I finally am pure," she said softly.

Jesus had wiped away the shame of all those years and brought Shana the healing she had longed for. He had brought truth to bear on her situation, and she had received it. Something supernatural had taken place. Shana walked with her head high after that. She understood that the Lord had cleansed her and set her free. She realized she was precious to Him. She was His, and she was pure.

It is true that once we give our hearts to the Lord, we begin new and fresh. Without Him, our efforts to steer our ships clear of the rocks can cause us shipwreck. Once we turn the vessel over to Him, He helps us navigate the rough waters.

Therefore if anyone is in Christ, he is a new creature; the old things passed away; behold, new things have come.

—2 Cor. 5:17

THE WOMAN AT THE WELL

Everyone who drinks of this water will thirst again; but whoever drinks of the water that I will give him shall never thirst; but the water that I will give him **will become in him a well of water springing up to eternal life.**

—John 4:13

She was a Samaritan woman drawing water from a well when Jesus found her. He simply asked her for a drink. This astonished her for the Jews had no dealings with Samaritans. "Who is this man?" she must have wondered. She was a woman with a past, heartbroken by many relationships, and living with a man who would not marry her. She had been abused, discarded, and loved all within her short lifetime. Who was this man whose eyes seemed to pierce her with their love and kindness? She was sure that she had been forgotten by any god.

He had promised her living water. "What is the source of this living water?" she must have wondered. Yet she knew she longed for this very thing. God had not forgotten her; He had sent His Son to reconcile the world to Himself. She was conversing with Jesus, the Messiah. The King of Kings and Lord of Lords revealed Himself to her.

If you knew the gift of God, and who it is who says to you, "Give Me a drink," you would have asked Him, and He would have given you living water.

—John 4:10

BELOVED

How beautiful you are, my darling, how beautiful you are! Your eyes are like doves behind your veil; Your hair....Your teeth.

—Song of Songs 4:1-2

In Mike Bickle's Song of Songs series, he describes this unique love we have for Jesus and He for us. Once we catch a glimpse of His heart, there is no turning back. In Song of Songs, we, the beloved, are referred to as having dove's eyes. "How beautiful you are, my darling. How beautiful you are! Your eyes are like doves" (Song of Songs 1:15).

And then later:

> O my dove, in the clefts of the rock, in the secret place of the steep pathway, let me see your form, let me hear your voice; for your voice is sweet, and your form is lovely.
>
> —Song of Songs 2:14

Until we finally hear, "Your eyes are like doves behind your veil" (Song of Songs 4:1). But why are we called doves? What is so significant about them to Jesus? Let's look at a few parallels together.

Doves have no peripheral vision; they can only focus on what their eyes behold before them. They gaze at each other without being distracted. Rather, they offer their whole-hearted affection to each other. The parallel is clear: once we behold Jesus, it is His face we seek, and His love captivates us.[26] Once we behold Him, we have eyes only for Him.

On my way to work one day, I saw two doves on the side of the road. One seemed to be staring at me curiously, so I paused to observe the scene. I shall never forget it: the male dove was standing beside his mate who had been partially crushed by a car. As his mate's feathers blew in the breeze, my heart was stirred. Here before me was a picture of our love for Jesus and His love in turn for us. He would not leave the side of His beloved; it was a covenant. So too is ours. These doves are single-minded and loyal creatures who demonstrate their love for their beloved. And this is how Christ views us.

Jesus, Himself, in turn is said to have dove's eyes for us. Song of Songs 5:12 states, "His eyes are like doves beside streams of water, bathed in milk." Jesus' longing and affection are returned to the degree that, "You have made my heart beat faster My heart, My sister, My bride: You have made my heart beat faster with one look of your eyes, with one link of your necklace" (Song of Songs 4:9).

Imagine that one glance of my eyes ravishes the heart of the King! How can this be? His heart swoons, and He cherishes me. My heart moves Him. He is a personal God who cares for the whole person. He is my rescuer, and He sees my affection.

Chapter 9

Captivating

You are a garden spring, a well of fresh water, and streams flowing from Lebanon.

—Song of Solomon 4:15

WE ARE A "spring sealed up," Song of Solomon 4:12 states. Just as a garden set apart only for the King, so are we a fountain, our hearts sealed. According to *The New John Gill Exposition of the Entire Bible*,

> The allusion may be to the sealed fountains great personages reserved for their own use; such as the kings of Persia had, of which the king and his eldest son only might drink; and King Solomon might have such a spring and fountain in his garden, either at Jerusalem or at Ethan, where he had pleasant gardens, in which he took great delight.[27]

Thus, there is the image of that spring of crystal-clear water from which only the King drinks. It is a garden reserved just for Him, which in the Jewish writings reflected the chastity of the bride.[28]

ALTOGETHER LOVELY

Consecrate yourselves therefore, and be holy; for I am holy.

—Lev. 11:44b

The summer after graduating from college, I went to work at a family-owned summer camp in Florida. The staff was cheerful. The camp featured horseback riding, sailing, and roller skating as the three primary forms of recreation. Each evening we saw a gorgeous sunset over the lake. Since the children's experiences were for the most part positive, parents routinely sent their children there year after year.

After our orientation, I was assigned, with another counselor, to live with and mentor ten thirteen-year-old girls. This was a task in and of itself. They were delightful brown and blonde-haired, green-eyed and brown-eyed girls on the brink of womanhood. Most were sweet, innocent, and precious in their own way.

Although the boys and girls attending the camp were well disciplined, an occasional bad apple tried to spoil the bunch. Rumors spread of a couple that had moonlight trysts on the beach at night, and another young man (twelve years old) who had deflowered a girl in the lavatory. Naturally, he had been counseled and sent home. Fortunately, these few were the exceptions, not the rule.

Still, I sat down one evening to share my heart with the girls about the importance of purity and waiting on God's timing. Although it was not a Christian camp, God had opened the door wide to minister and sow His words of life into these girls. We talked about how our bodies are temples, and that becoming one with someone can only lead to heartbreak unless that union ends in marriage. "Once you become one flesh with someone, there is a tearing that takes place if you separate," I said. The girls nodded in agreement, as I pleaded with them not to go out alone with any young man after dark.

All went well until one night a week before camp ended. Susan, the other counselor for our house, had the day off, so I was alone with the girls that night. In the middle of the night, I was awakened from a dead sleep by whispering and the sound of footsteps. Up in a flash, I hopped out of bed and flicked on the light. The backdoor, located next to the bathroom, was swinging open and shut, so I quickly shut it. Were the boys trying to get into the cabin? Locking it was not an option as the wood had warped and the hook would not quite reach. I returned to the main bedroom. All the girls were still in their beds. I could do nothing but marvel at this. Perhaps they had tried to sneak out and were afraid to be caught. I again reaffirmed that God loved them, as did I, and that each and everyone was valuable. "Giving your affections away to one of these boys would lead to further heartache," I had counseled.

To ensure we were not disturbed any further that night, I placed a trash can just outside the backdoor as an alarm should anyone try to sneak out with the boys. Although I could not get the backdoor to lock, the door did have ledges on it, where I skillfully placed the dozen shampoo bottles the girls were using. I did this with great joy as I reached over the shower door for any remaining bottles of shower gel.

Satisfied, I returned to my top bunk by the front door. Moments later, I heard the crashing of the trashcan outside and the loud thudding of a dozen shampoo bottles. Stunned, I rose and flashed on the light. Miraculously, all the girls were still in their beds. "What is happening?" I wondered, getting out of bed for the second time.

Upon entering the bathroom, I was greeted by an open back door and Pantene bottles strewn everywhere. Shutting the door behind me, I asked God for strength and wisdom. Suddenly an idea came to me. For three weeks, I had suffered as the girls had played hard rock music endlessly during our down time; seven of the ten had brought their own boom boxes with them.

"All right," I said, borrowing Chloe's boom box, "I have listened to y'all's music from the beginning. Now it's time to listen to mine. I'll stop playing this whenever someone lets me know what is going on." And so, Beethoven's Fifth Symphony began. I deliberately paused in front of each girl's bunk so she could have the full effect at three in the morning.

Finally, I got the response I needed. "Tell her," Karen, their leader said groggily from underneath her pillow. Erin was the first to respond.

Apparently, three boys had snuck in trying to get my girls to follow them to the lake. One had crawled up to Erin's top bunk to wake her, only to hear her refusal. "We did what you asked. We did not want to leave with them," Erin said.

She had apparently been fighting with her guy when I arose and turned on the lights. Swiftly, he had hidden himself underneath her blanket at the bottom of her bunk. Another boy had been cornered between two bunks while Cheryl quickly threw a blanket on top of him. The third guy had hidden himself behind the wooden door in the shower—the place where all the scorpions came out at night. I can only imagine his heart racing as I reached over his head time and again retrieving shampoo bottles.

"Okay, girls," I said. "You know I love you and care about you. That is why this is such a big deal." I paused. "I am so proud of you for staying," I said almost through tears. Then, changing gears to deal with the matter at hand, I asked firmly, "Now, who are these young men? They will have to be disciplined." When everything was settled, we all went to sleep, thankful for God's protection and for their desire to remain pure.

> Put me like a seal over your heart, like a seal on your arm. For love is as strong as death.
>
> —Song of Solomon 8:6

A Treasured Possession

> My beloved is mine, and I am his.
>
> —Song of Solomon 2:16

Nardoi is the Greek word used not only in the passage regarding Mary's gift to Jesus, but is also seen throughout the Song of Solomon in 1:12, 4:13-14.[29] According to the *International Standard Bible Encyclopedia*, nard was very precious and costly. This brought me great joy as I discovered a parallel with Jesus' description of us, His bride.

> A garden locked is my sister, *my* bride, a rock garden locked, a spring sealed up. Your shoots are an orchard of pomegranates with choice fruits, henna and **nard** plants, **nard** and saffron, calamus and cinnamon, with all the trees of frankincense, myrrh and aloes, along with **all the finest spices**. You are a garden spring, a well of fresh water, and streams flowing from Lebanon.
>
> —Song of Solomon 4:12-14

Here, we as believers are compared to a garden, but not simply any garden—*a King's garden*. We are so precious to Him that we are reserved only for Him. Commentators agree:

Likely that the allusion is to a garden near Jerusalem, called the king's garden, Adrichomius makes mention of, which was shut up, and only for the king's use and pleasure: to which the church may be compared… by the sovereign grace of God.[30]

But there is more. What is in this garden set apart for the King to walk in? It is a place where only the finest and choicest of plants are grown, including the precious nard.

To these saints may be compared, because pleasant and delightful, of a sweet smell, and rare and excellent…having pleasant and precious plants of great renown; or consisting of persons of different gifts and graces; in whose hearts… are sown or planted and raised up by the Spirit of God…as in a garden, the plants are watered with the grace of God; the trees of righteousness are pruned by Christ's father, the vinedresser; the fences are kept up, and the whole is watched over night and day.[31]

SET APART

Are you starting to feel precious to the Lord? He sees you and me as valuable to Him. And not only that, but He takes special care to ensure that we are watched over and protected. We are a delightful place that He longs to go.

And here Christ, the owner of it, takes his delightful walks, and grants his presence with his people. And the church is like an "enclosed" garden; for distinction, being separated by the grace of God, in election, redemption, effectual calling… and for protection, being encompassed with the power of God, as a wall about it.[32]

So the Lord walks into the fragrant garden of our hearts that has been planted and watered by His Father.

Priceless

My beloved responded and said to me, "Arise, my darling, my beautiful one, and come along. For behold, the winter is past, the rain is over and gone. The flowers have already appeared in the land; the time has arrived for pruning the vines, and the voice of the turtledove has been heard in our land. The fig tree has ripened its figs, and the vines in blossom have given forth their fragrance. Arise, my darling, my beautiful one, and come along!"

—Song of Solomon 2:10-13

A DANCE IN THE DESERT

LIKE ALL OF us, she was wandering in search of something, coming close but never quite reaching it. Sometimes she felt it almost between her fingertips like silk fabric, only to have it slip from her grasp. Reaching...always reaching. Just a little behind the movement of this dance. "There must be more," she reasoned. But what? And where? This emptiness in her soul persisted as she drifted from entertainment to entertainment—from one to another.

Searching...searching...dancing to music she could hear only in her heart, but never finding the right partner. From a distance she saw one. Hope arose in her heart. Finally...could it be this one? She raced toward him only to realize once she arrived that it was only a silhouette of what she hoped for. She was again off to the next one.

Finally, exhausted, she softened like a tender branch, bowing to the floor. Resting, recovering her breath, she saw Him. He had been there all along...waiting. Wondering when she would see Him. She had been rushing past Him in search of her other lovers. Now she sees only Him.

He speaks to her, softly, gently. Caressing her cheek, He unveils the mystery. She is His. Her eyes behold His. His gaze is mesmerizing. She cannot speak; only listen. She is overwhelmed. "I hedged you in," he says, smiling gently. And He begins to reveal the meaning she had searched for all along. She hears Him speak words of truth. Like a tree drinking from streams of living water, she soaks in His presence. She is no longer alone or lonely. The hole is filled. For the first moment in her life, the void, the meaninglessness, has been filled. She understands.

YOUR CHAMPION

Thrust into the middle of the crowd, a woman with a similar plight must have felt humiliated. Still naked with only the barest of clothes to cover her, she trembled, awaiting judgment. Would anyone show mercy? Where was her lover? Was there no one to intercede? They would stone her; this was certain. She had been caught in the very act of adultery.

> Jesus saw her as valuable.

And then Jesus arose, and one by one her accusers left. Finally, He came to her and gently said, "Woman, where are they? Did no one condemn you?' She said, 'No one, Lord.' And Jesus said, 'I do not condemn you, either. Go from now on sin no more'" (John 8:10-11). She had been given a second chance.

IN SEARCH OF...

Most women desire a man who will be a covering for them, someone who will protect them from the coming storms. Yet the woman in John 8 was left alone to face her accusers—that is, until Jesus intervened. He did not condone her actions; what the woman caught in adultery did was sinful with consequences that hurt her and hurt the man with whom she was involved. But most importantly, her actions broke the heart of God.

Jesus imperatively stated, "Go from now on sin no more." And therein lies the key. Sin causes incredible brokenness and pain. It is true that the Ten Commandments were designed for our own protection. God laid them out so that we might experience the full expression of His love on earth. For good reason, adultery and covetousness are listed among the things we should not do.

Committing adultery had caused this woman brokenness in her spirit. She had become one flesh with another person with whom she could not spend the rest of her life. "**And the two shall become one flesh; so they are no longer two, but one flesh**" (Mark 10:8). Imagine sharing intimate moments and conversations with someone you love, knowing you will never be able to be with that person again. (According to Dr. Linda Mintle, most men do not marry the woman with whom they had an affair.) She had given of herself and placed herself in the most precarious situation. Was she in love with him? If so, she could not be loved in return.

> Every other sin that a man commits is outside the body, but the immoral man sins against his own body. Or do you not know that your body is a temple of the Holy Spirit who is in you, whom you have from God, and that you are not your own? For you have been bought with a price: therefore glorify God in your body.
> —1 Cor. 6:18-20

Jesus forgave this woman caught in adultery; she got a second chance. He stood by her. He was not embarrassed. There would be no more guilt or shame, if she would turn from her sin. In spite of the grave charges leveled against her, Jesus offered her a chance for cleansing. If she repented, she could begin again with a clean slate. In the Greek, the word *metanoeo* means to change one's mind for the better and to amend with abhorrence one's past sins.[33] Her past would not mar her future if she received this gift offered to her and if she walked in purity—if she could turn from her sin and begin anew.

The sanctuary of marriage can best be explained as living in the will of God behind the protective walls of a castle. Behind the protective walls, a couple experiences the blessing of God, peace, and intimacy, without shame. The palace walls are high and meant to keep out the enemy. If one commits adultery, it is like deliberately stepping outside the walls where the enemy is waiting to do harm. Unless there is repentance, the safety offered evaporates.

> But thanks be to God that though you were slaves of sin, you became obedient from the heart to that form of teaching to which you were committed, and having been freed from sin, you became slaves of righteousness.
>
> —Rom. 6:17-18

YOU ARE LOVELY

Then why would this woman enter into adultery with a man she could never marry? For a woman, according to Eldredge in her book, *Captivating,* the question is one of beauty and value.[34] It is true that if a young girl is told that she is beautiful and is loved by her father, she is less likely to become involved in promiscuous relationships.[35] She will not be as easily moved when a young man pays her such compliments. She knows that she is valuable, and does not need this reinforced by a man. Again, it comes down to knowing the truth about our identities in Christ and how valuable we are to God. He sees us so much differently than we see ourselves sometimes.

> You are as **beautiful** as Tirzah, my darling, as lovely as Jerusalem, as awesome as an army with banners.
>
> —Song of Solomon 6:4

God designed marriage to parallel His unconditional love for us. Marriage was designed to be God's best expression of love for us. In it, we experience intimacy without shame, along with commitment, faithfulness, and love. Oh, the majesty! According to Focus on the Family's series entitled, *The Truth Project,* God designed marriage to mirror the intimacy experienced in the Trinity. The Book of Ephesians compels us.

Husbands, love your wives, just as Christ also loved the church and gave Himself up for her, so that He might sanctify her, having cleansed her by the by the washing of water and the word, that He might present to Himself the church in all her glory.

—Eph. 5:25-27

As we explore these passages, it becomes evident that God modeled our relationship and fellowship within the family unit after the communion experienced in the Godhead.[36]

In love, God established covenant. Love is meant to be a beautiful expression of love between a man and woman who make a covenant to love one another forever. Adultery breaks that covenant and is the ultimate betrayal. It takes grace to keep the fires burning at home for a lifetime, but it is possible. I would recommend the film *Fireproof* and the book, *The Love Dare,* as they practically touch on this theme.

LONGING FOR LOVE

Around the middle of the eighth century B.C. a man arose who would paint a picture of God's unconditional love for His covenant people. Hosea was an honorable man, a prophet. At God's request, he took as his wife a woman who was not faithful. Her name was Gomer, and she was greatly pursued by her husband. To read a beautiful portrayal of their relationship in modern terms, I would highly recommend *Redeeming Love* by Francine Rivers.

Just as God reached out to the Israelites, letting them know of His great love for them, so Hosea reached out to Gomer. At first, she spurned him, trusting in her other lovers. Yet, no matter how far she ran from him, he pursued her, desiring only her.

Therefore, behold, I will hedge up her way with thorns, and I will build a wall against her so that she cannot find her paths. She will pursue her lovers, but she will not overtake them; and she will seek them, but will not find them. Then she will say, "I will go back to my first husband, for it is better for me then than now!"

—Hosea 2:6-7

Misty Edwards sings a lovely ballad that complements this passage.

You hedge me in with thorns all around me,
the fragrance of a rose…
the fragrance of love.
You hedge me in with thorns all around me,
the fragrance of a rose…
the fragrance of jealousy.
Where could I go?
Where could I hide?
Where can I run from you, O God?[37]

Truly, no matter where we run to, we can never run outside the circle of His arms. God desires us for Himself. He is as jealous for us as a husband is for his wife. As Allen Hood has stated, "If you are married and truly love your wife, you would never share her with another."[38] Your covenant is sacred. She is yours, and you are hers. It is like that with God; He does not desire us to give ourselves to false idols when *He* is the source of all life. We are sacred to Him.

You must hear this, "He *loves* you. He loves *you*. *He* loves you." He desires your heart in surrender. He will not break it; you can trust Him. Rather, He will treasure your heart, nurturing and protecting you as no other lover could. His arms are safe. Beloved, run to Him; His arms are open wide.

Chapter 11

Safe in the Arms of Love

As for God, His way is perfect; the word of the Lord is proven; He is a shield to all who trust in Him.

—Ps. 18:30 NKJV

YOUR HIDING PLACE

SHE WAS A pretty girl with long, dark tresses covering her small frame like a cloak as she bent over to fill the bucket with water. She would need to tidy up while it was still light. Her home was a small one, built into the very walls of the city. Pushing back a strand of hair from her face, she spied two new guests approaching. Her gray eyes studied them with caution. Standing up to her full height, she advanced toward the door. Something in one of the men's green eyes made her heart melt like wax inside of her. His countenance appeared peaceful and kind, yet holy. Who were these men?

They said they needed a place to stay, lodging for the night. Demurely, she set before them a simple meal. They ate gratefully, the green-eyed one's gaze meeting hers as she swept and tidied. There was something so different about them. Their eyes were filled with hope… and kindness. Could it be that they were…Israelites? She had heard the stories of how their God had parted the Red Sea before them and had given them tremendous victory over Sihon and Og. Everywhere they went their God gave them success. Destruction met those who resisted them. She was in awe. The fear of the Lord came upon her.

Turning toward her front window, she saw a strange man scurry away down the street in quite a hurry. He was wearing rags, all in tatters. As he glanced over his shoulder, she saw his face. Something in his eyes told her the call had gone out. If these men were who she thought they were, they would soon be discovered. This would fetch quite a price from the king, she mused. She turned back to face the two men. Their eyes looked at hers expectantly. She reverenced this God of theirs. What should she do? Her eyes flashed open wide. The flax! Hurriedly, she escorted them to the roof.

She heard the rumbling of the horses' hooves before she ever saw them. The king of Jericho's men, a mass of angry, fierce warriors, dismounted and moved purposefully toward her tiny abode. Steeling herself for what was to come, Rahab stood in the doorframe barring their way at first. She put into play every seductive trick she had learned over the years. Appearing attractively bored, she leaned back gracefully against the doorframe, stretched out like a cat awakening from her nap. One of the men, roughly pushing aside another man in his path, came face to face with Rahab. "Bring out the men who have come to you, who have entered your house, for they have come to search out all the land" (Josh. 2:3).

Appearing to acquiesce to the man's thundering, Rahab raised her eyebrows, appearing somewhat alarmed by his words. She replied:

> Yes, the men came to me, but I did not know where they were from. It came about when it was time to shut the gate at dark, that the men went out; I do not know where the men went. Pursue them quickly, for you will overtake them.
>
> —Josh. 2:4-5

Her last few words were urgent and encouraging. Grumbling, the men quickly turned again toward their horses. The diversion had worked, for the men of Jericho left the city in hot pursuit of the Israelites hoping to overtake them on the road to Jordan. They had no idea the two spies were safely resting beneath the flax on the roof of Rahab's house for: "The woman had taken the two men and hidden them" (Josh. 2:4).

After the king's men left, Rahab crept back to the roof. Before the Israelites lay down to rest, she spoke to them:

> I know that the Lord has given you the land, and that the terror of you has fallen on us, and all the inhabitants of the land have melted away before you.... for the Lord your God, He is God in heaven above and on earth beneath. Now therefore, please swear to me by the Lord, since I have dealt kindly with you, that you also will deal kindly with my father's household, and give me a pledge of truth, and spare my father and my mother and my brothers and my sisters, with all who belong to them.
> —Josh. 2:9, 11-13

The men agreed, saying, "Our life for yours if you do not tell this business of ours; and it shall come about when the Lord gives us the land that we will deal kindly and faithfully with you" (Josh. 2:14). And so it was decided.

To help the men escape, Rahab threw a rope out her window and let the men down since the city's gates were shut. She advised them to "Go to the hill country, so that the pursuers will not happen upon you, and hide yourselves there for three days" (Josh. 2:16). And so they did. But before parting, they asked her to hang a scarlet cord out of that very window so that when they returned to the land, her household might be spared. Rahab agreed, gathering all her family into the house when the Israelites returned to conquer Jericho.

Rahab did a very courageous thing. She hid the men under the flax on the roof in order to protect them. Thus, when the Israelites returned to claim the area of Jericho, she and her household were spared. But there is more to the story than at first meets the eye, for Rahab is also written into a very precious lineage—that of Christ.

> The record of the genealogy of Jesus the Messiah, the son of David, the son of Abraham. Salmon was the father of Boaz by Rahab, Boaz was the father of Obed by Ruth, and Obed the father of Jesse. Jesse was the father of David the king. David was the father of Solomon by Bathsheba who had been the wife of Uriah.
> —Matt. 1:1, 5-6

Scholars speculate as to whether or not Salmon was in fact one of the spies Rahab harbored. If he indeed was, he had a chance to meet and fall in love with this woman at the very moment she acknowledged and chose to serve God.

Salmon's love for Rahab prepared his son, Boaz, to receive his wife, Ruth. Ruth was a foreigner, a Moabite, and a widow. Yet Boaz never hesitated to marry one such as she, having watched his father treat his mother with such respect and love. Given the way Boaz esteemed Ruth, one can only guess that his father Salmon had cherished Rahab. She may have felt discarded by others as a prostitute, but, after Jericho, she never felt discarded by God. I can imagine Boaz as a child watching his parents interact with each other.

Thus, God prepared the ground, and proved Himself faithful as their Redeemer. He is faithful to take the pains and impurities and wash them away, if we will but open our hearts to let love lead the way.

> For the LORD God is a sun and shield; The LORD gives grace and glory;
> No **good thing** does He withhold from those who walk uprightly.
> —Ps. 84:11

Beloved, I may not know all that you have gone through, but I do know that there is a God who forgives you and who is willing to see you cleansed—made new and pure. The past does not hold a candle to the hopeful future that He lays before you. Rahab feared God and it was counted to her as righteousness. She revered and reverenced Him. And God in His infinite mercy wove for her a beautiful tapestry of His love reflected in her story.

Leave the broken past in His hands, and step out into the golden sunshine with Him. He sent His Son Jesus to make all things new. Beloved, leave the ashes of yesterday, and allow Him to clothe you in the robes of His righteousness. He is waiting with arms open wide.

> To grant those who mourn in Zion, giving them a garland instead of ashes, the oil of gladness instead of mourning, the mantle of praise instead of a spirit of fainting. So they will be called oaks of righteousness, the planting of the Lord, that He may be glorified.
> —Isa. 61:3

He Allures Her

> Therefore, behold, I will allure her, bring her into the wilderness and speak kindly to her.
> —Hosea 2:14

In the Book of Hosea, we learn that God draws us to a place where we can be still before Him. This wilderness is the place of encounter.[39] It is the place where the Lord alone can comfort. Consumed by love, He removes other things that seek to take the place of His comfort. He hedges us in and protects us as He becomes the comforter of our souls. It is there that He speaks tenderly to us, quieting the voices and noises until we are silent before Him.

John the Baptist went to the wilderness to hear the Bridegroom. It equipped him to love God for the rest of his life.[40] When we hear the voice of the Bridegroom, He fills our barrenness with signs of life.

> Who is this coming up from the wilderness, leaning on her beloved?
> —Song of Solomon 8:5

Awakened to Love

Dana Candler gave a powerful testimony of God's great love for us at a conference held at the International House of Prayer. The battle for us is, "Who can win the affection of the human heart?" Once we surrender our lives to Him, we have said the big "*Yes*" to Jesus. We have essentially said "yes" to love. But there is more to come. For each day after that, when our choices mirror the choices of His heart, we are choosing Him in the smaller things. We are saying "yes" to love and "no" to seduction.[41] Every time after that, when He enables us to triumph over an addiction, weakness, or area of bondage, we come into victory. Each time we surrender to His will, it releases in us a greater fragrance of a glorious person named Jehovah.[42]

> Awake, O north wind, and come, wind of the south; Make my garden breathe out fragrance, let its spices be wafted abroad. May my beloved come into his garden and eat its choice fruits!
> —Song of Solomon 4:16

MY BELOVED CALLS

He brings us to the place where our hearts are ready to say "Yes." It is true that we wish Him to, "kiss me with the kisses of your mouth! For Your love is better than wine" (Song of Solomon 1:2). The mouth speaks of intimacy. We reach a point where we desire Him more than anything else. And He has brought us to this place.

According to Bickle, Jesus is motivating the church, His Bride, by what He sees at the end of the age. He calls forth her budding virtues before they come to pass. He sees us at the end of the journey, and He does not doubt His ability to bring us there. She is coming out of the wilderness leaning in strong love on her Beloved. (See Song of Solomon 8:5.)

> Mary then took a pound of very costly perfume of pure nard, and anointed the feet of Jesus and wiped His feet with her hair; and the house was filled with the fragrance of the perfume.
> —John 12:3

This is another passage that speaks of the sweet fragrance of perfume. Its context is slightly different in that Mary had been a follower of Jesus for some time. Unlike the woman in the previous passage mentioned, Mary had already come to the place of repentance. Thus, this gift was an outpouring of her love for Jesus and possibly her gratitude to Him for raising Lazarus, her brother, from the dead.

Matthew Henry's Concise Commentary elaborates:

> Mary gave a token of love to Christ, who had given real tokens of his love to her and her family. God's Anointed should be our Anointed. Has God poured on him the oil of gladness above his fellows, let us pour on him the ointment of our best affections.[43]

Mary took the best that she had and bathed Jesus' feet in the sweet and costly perfume as He reclined at the table. Just so, our lives are offerings to the Lord.

> While the king was at his table, my perfume gave forth its fragrance.
> —Song of Solomon 1:12

Chapter 12

Transformed by Love

You shall increase their gladness; they will be glad in Your presence as with the gladness of the harvest.

—Isa. 9:3

TENDER TO HIS TOUCH

AS A YOUNG professor, I have been privileged to witness what happens when God bathes people in His love. They are transformed. It is destined to occur. Chiquita was no exception. Stubborn, sassy, and sitting in the front row, Chiquita quipped, "Professor..." She paused, searching for the words. "Joy," I finished for her, smiling. Since most students don't remember their teachers' names until later in the semester, I was accustomed to this loss for words. She smiled back, "Why you make that last test so hard?"

Chiquita was a piece of work. A mother at the age of sixteen, she had learned how to cope the fast way. Now twenty-two, she had enrolled in school in the hope of finding a better job to support her growing family. *That tough exterior was a mask for the world of hurt she has been through,* I thought.

She sat beside two other classmates who were in the same boat as she was. Together, they were a disruptive bunch, always interrupting the class with impish comments and derogatory remarks. It wore on me after a while. "What shall I do, Lord?" I moaned. It had taken me a while to get used to the fact that in the middle of lecture, a student might jump in with a comment completely unrelated to the topic at hand. Until now, most of them had been harmless and conversational, like Paisley's, "Where you get that dress at, Professor Joy? Girl, that's sweet! Professor Joy stylin'." And Paisley rolled her head while the class laughingly agreed. I had to smile; they were trying to have a conversation with me. The class was a dialogue for them, not a monologue.

Chiquita's comments had been more challenging, almost intimidating. Egged on by her friends' snickers, she deliberately undermined my authority. Gently, the Lord opened my eyes. "She's been hurt, Joy...very badly. Treat her with respect...and always with love," the still small voice cautioned. "Okay," I replied, "Lord, please show me how to love her and give me patience. I need Your wisdom to maneuver through this. Teach me to lead with love."

Throughout the whole semester, God inspired me to honor Chiquita. I remember viewing one of Dr. Gary Smalley's videos on strengthening relationships. He stated that we should see the word "Stradivarius" stamped on the heads of those we care for, symbolizing their priceless nature. Each person is created in the image of God; we should be in awe and remember this in greeting one another.

In addition to honoring her, my responses to her quips also changed. Instead of being frustrated, I lovingly teased her back. At first, this surprised her, but eventually we developed a rapport. Then, gradually, Chiquita began to soften in her attitude toward me. She was learning to trust.

I will never forget the day that this transformation was complete. I was passing back papers, when I glanced up to give Chiquita hers. It was after we had finished the commemorative speeches where students shared from their hearts and became more transparent through their speeches.

For the first time, I saw her as the little girl she once was. There was no malice in her face this time, just innocence. She was like a ten-year-old girl in a classroom looking up at her teacher, no cares about the world outside.

It was a defining moment for me. God had broken through. As she beheld me, I tearfully smiled. She had about her an air of dignity now.

The world had treated her harshly, and she had responded in kind. Yet, God saw her differently. He saw her as the beautiful woman she was created to be. Moved profoundly, I was able to witness it too. He knows the end from the beginning. He sees us as we will be.

FOREVER CHANGED

He was zealous. He was notorious. He was well known for traveling from house to house and arresting men and women alike. His threats were murderous and his intent real. He was passionate...about the wrong things...until one day.

> As he was traveling, it happened that he was approaching Damascus, and suddenly a light from heaven flashed around him; and he fell to the ground and heard a voice saying to him, "Saul, Saul, why are you persecuting Me?" And he said, "Who are You, Lord?" And He said, "I am Jesus whom you are persecuting, but get up and enter the city, and it will be told you what you must do."
>
> —Acts 9:3-6

For three days, Paul remained blind until God sent a man named Ananias to pray for him. Having heard of Paul's reputation, Ananias hesitated until the Lord spoke these words to him. "Go, for he is a chosen instrument of Mine, to bear My name before the Gentiles and kings and the sons of Israel" (Acts 9:15).

Paul went on to share the gospel throughout the world as a great missionary. He was beaten with rods, whipped, stoned, and shipwrecked, yet his passion for Jesus never waivered (2 Cor. 11:24-33). He had encountered the truth: love in its purest form, and he was compelled to tell the world about it. God transformed his zeal into something life giving.

THE POWER OF "I'M SORRY"

> God causes all things to work together for good to those who love God, to those who are called according to His purpose.
>
> —Rom. 8:28

Rick was a dark-haired youth with a fun sense of humor. Although he sat in the back of the class most days, his presence was always felt. Since it was the first class of the day, I sometimes found myself rushing to get to class on time. At the time, it was a forty-minute commute at six-thirty in the morning.

I don't remember why I felt so stressed that particular morning, but I know the class noticed. I was reviewing material for an upcoming test, but the students were not responding to any of my questions. I felt as if I were "throwing it out there, but nothing was coming back." Frustrated and tired from the early morning push, I snapped, "It would be great if you guys would help me out a little."

Since this kind of comment was unlike me, the class was puzzled. Rick, it turned out, was offended. Although I apologized the next time we met, Rick was not there to hear the apology. "Lord, what do I do?" I asked. A gentle voice responded to my spirit's cry. "Rick has been hurt by authority figures in his life. You need to apologize to him directly and admit that you were wrong to lash out like that. And he needs to forgive you." "Okay," I said.

Often, a father figure or close family member has hurt the student by misusing or abusing power. This can leave the family member with a lasting scar and an innate mistrust of those in direct authority. God loves to heal such wounds, if only we let Him. I know. I have walked through situations with both healthy leaders who longed to see me reach my potential, and unhealthy ones who wounded me by their actions. Acknowledging the sin committed against us and forgiving the other person is one of the first steps to total healing.

When Rick returned to class a week later, I pulled him aside. "Rick," I said slowly, "I apologized to the class on Wednesday. But since you were not present, I wanted to let you know personally that I am so sorry for taking out my frustrations on you guys last Monday. It was not your fault. I was just having a rough day. Will you forgive me?" Rick looked at me in stunned silence. He could tell that I meant it. I was a little teary-eyed at this point. "Yes, of course," he said. "Everyone has rough days." I smiled in gratitude, "Thanks."

From that point on, Rick was not only on time for every class; he was fifteen minutes early. His attitude had also changed; Rick listened thoughtfully to what I said as I taught. Sensing a deep sense of respect growing, I thanked God. He had taught me something valuable: Admitting you are wrong closes the door of offense. According to Dr. Gary Smalley, a counselor for more than thirty-five years, one of children's greatest complaints against their parents is that they fail to admit when they are wrong.

> Give, and it will be given to you. They will pour into your lap a good measure—pressed down, shaken together, and running over.
> —Luke 6:38

CLOSE CALL

> For everyone will be salted with fire. Salt is good; but if salt becomes unsalty, with what will you make it salty again? Have salt in yourselves, and be at peace with one another.
> —Mark 9:49-50

Chris was an earnest student. The dark-haired sophomore seemed polite and attentive throughout the class lectures. As we prepared for our persuasive speeches, he pulled me aside after class. "Professor Joy," he said, "I was wondering if I could personalize my topic for the next speech."

"Of course," I replied thoughtfully, "What did you have in mind?"

He then highlighted a few thoughts he had on the topic of drunk driving. "What a great topic for this class to learn more about, Chris! Yes, there are people who will hear your speech and think twice before getting into a car after drinking or with someone who has been drinking." I added, "This has the potential to save a life." He nodded in agreement and I waited for his speech. Although Chris had shared with me a rough idea of the scope of his presentation, I was fully unprepared for the testimony he was going to give.

Like many teenagers, Chris had experimented with alcohol in high school. "It had been fun," he said, "hanging out with his friends and partying," he paused. "That is until one night."

Chris and his buddies had been driving home from a party late one Saturday night. Meanwhile, on a dark, country road, an elderly lady was returning home from visiting some friends. *CRASH!* The two cars collided. Hilda's car was T-boned. Chris had hit her car on the passenger side. Fortunately, Chris and his friends suffered only minor injuries since the air bags deployed swiftly. Hilda, however, was not so lucky. She had survived, but endured excruciating pain in the hospital where Chris seldom left her bedside.

Sadly, due to the circumstances, Chris owed $100,000 for the accident, court costs, and all of the physical therapy that was involved for Hilda. This shocked me. "Is he bankrupt?" I wondered.

Chris had taken responsibility for his own actions and was not shirking in any way. He had changed in a positive way because of it. This nineteen-year-old boy was speaking with the calm and confident maturity of someone much older. I greatly admired and respected him for this. In an age where most people would take the easy way out, he had faced the consequences.

In fact, Chris had built a relationship with Hilda over the course of her recovery. He showed us pictures of her throughout her recuperation. It was easy to see that the two had become friends. Hilda had forgiven him.

I watched the impact his testimony had on his audience. I hope and pray that before any of them turned the key in the ignition again, they would remember Chris and his story. To this day, I admire the humble young man who had the courage to do what was right.

> For God has not given us a spirit of timidity, but of power and love and discipline.
>
> —2 Timothy 1:7

A Tough Exterior

In the early days of my teaching career, I had the privilege of teaching at a local community college located in the heart of the downtown area. There the student population consisted of a mixture of single mothers returning to school, reformed gang members, and adults seeking certification or a degree that would enable them to change careers. In this challenging environment, God broke through and touched lives. One of them was mine.

Billy was a tough-looking kid, about twenty years old. Wearing faded blue jeans and a leather jacket to ward off the cold winter weather, he arrived at class the first day. I could tell that he was excited to be there; perhaps even more so than the other students. After a few weeks, however, I noticed him beginning to doze off a little in class.

One day, I motioned for another student to nudge him gently. He awoke, and noting his embarrassment, I smiled good-naturedly and said, "It is all good, Mr. Rivers. We are just glad to have you back." Nevertheless, I could sense from his expression that he was genuinely sorry to have slept through some of the material.

After class that day, Billy approached me respectfully. "Professor Joy, I'm sorry I dozed today. I started working the third shift so I can go to school, and this is my last class before I can go to sleep," he paused. "I used to run with gangs. I saw my cousin on the ground outside his house, first shot and then pushed from the second story. I found my brother and his best friend killed by gangs," he breathed, collecting his thoughts. "I don't want to be a part of that no more, Professor Joy. I want to go to school." He smiled, looking around the room. "This is my way out," he paused again, "If I stayed, I would have ended up dead too."

I nodded. Thinking it was a miracle he was still alive to tell this story. "Billy, I am proud of you," I said, overwhelmed by his heart of sincerity. "I will tell you what; you sleep all you want. I will just be sure to wake you up for all of the important parts," I winked. He laughed, and we hugged. As I watched him disappear to get that needed rest, I prayed and thanked God for protecting him thus far.

How precious is Your lovingkindness, O God! And the children of men take refuge in the shadow of Your wings.

—Ps. 36:7

Chapter 13

Hearing God's Voice

And the disciples were continually filled with joy and with the Holy
Spirit.

—Acts 13:52

BOOM

IT WAS A humbling experience to meet him. He was three-and-half-feet
tall if that, an expressive young man with sensitive, brown eyes. From
the time of his birth, Jorge had no legs—only a stump for one leg while
the other reached to where his knee should have been. Since he had no
arms as well, he had to pick up everything with his mouth.

He was a bright fellow with a heart to help others. One day, after
class, he hobbled over to me with a question. A look of concern flashed
across his face. He said he had been asked to give a speech at a middle
class pep rally and was unsure how to approach it. Laying my papers
aside, I asked, "What seems to be the trouble?

He began to pour out his story. "Well, *boom,* you see, Professor Joy.
I have been asked, *boom,* to share my testimony, *boom,* with these kids
and, *boom,* and I want to sound professional, *boom.* But I keep saying,
boom, throughout all my speeches." We both laughed.

Earlier that day, Jorge had given a speech before the class. When
he received the class' feedback sheets, he had been dismayed. Ellen, an

English teacher returning to school for re-certification, had marked off the number of times Jorge had said the word "*boom.*" Surprisingly, within the span of a five-minute speech, Jorge had used the word "*boom*" eighty-six times! In truth, I had actually debated whether to give him the sheet or not. In the long run, I knew it would benefit him. And so, immediately after class, Jorge approached me.

His pleading eyes met mine, "What can I do?" He was supposed to give his testimony at this rally. His heart's desire was to discourage these young kids from joining a gang. Jorge, who had once been looking for a place to belong, had himself been involved in a gang. Although I did not know all the details, I did know the consequences had been negative.

Now Jorge stood before me, desperate to know how to solve this vocalized pause issue. A vocalized pause is merely a filler such as "like," "um," or "er." It's meant to replace a pause as you transition from one point to the next and are gathering your thoughts.

I asked God for wisdom as to what to say. I truly didn't know what would be best. "Let's try this," I suggested. "I normally don't recommend this, but try writing out your speech exactly as you would say it without the "booms." Practice it and let's see if this helps you in your next in-class speech." Jorge agreed and just before he had to give his testimony before the middle school, he practiced his newly found skills on us.

His informative speech topic was on the drug Ecstasy. I was impressed with all of the statistics he presented along with a heartfelt plea not to try the drug. Just the physical effects alone were enough to convince anyone.

Then, suddenly, it happened. Right in the middle of Jorge's speech, he let a "boom" slip. He paused, panicked. "Yo! Yo! Yo!" he cried, scanning the room with his eyes. "I wish to retract that boom." Ellen held her pencil poised in mid-air. Jorge continued, "You see someone somewhere in this room is keeping track of the number of times I say it. I practiced this speech so I wouldn't say it. So please forget I ever said that 'boom.'"

Ellen and I smiled at each other across the room, and she did indeed drop her pencil. Jorge's speech was a success both in the classroom and at the school. I hope and pray that many lives were touched through his powerful testimony.

But you will receive power when the **Holy Spirit** has come upon you; and you shall be My witnesses both in Jerusalem, and in all Judea and Samaria, and even to the remotest part of the earth.

—Acts 1:8

Trusting

We must all learn to discern God's voice as He speaks to us through others, through His Word, and by His Spirit. His is that still small voice that speaks peace to the storm, comforts the brokenhearted, and makes the blind see.

Through the years, I learned to lean on my Beloved time and again as young students poured out their stories, presented a crisis, and cried on my shoulder. My life is a love song, and as the Father pours in, I pour out. Jesus went away to a quiet place to rest after ministering, and we, too, should follow His lead. There he speaks wisdom and restores our soul as only His love can.

Shout for joy, O heavens! And rejoice, O earth! Break forth into joyful shouting, O mountains! For the LORD has comforted His people and will have compassion on His afflicted.

—Isa. 49:13

When Words Matter Most

I remember Tiffany, a redheaded perfectionist in one of my early classes. Her papers and presentations exceeded all my expectations. One day she approached me, struggling for a topic for her next speech. "Professor Joy," she said, "I need your advice. I am trying to decide between two topics: art deco or how to assemble a wiccan altar. I was wondering if I could show the class how to set up an altar for witchcraft. If not, I can do art deco, since I am fascinated by it."

Needless to say, I was stunned. Trying hard not to show it, I silently prayed, "Give me grace and wisdom, Lord." Thankfully, these words came stumbling out of my mouth. "Hum, I would go with the art deco. Remember, you want to pick a topic with your audience in mind and that topic might appeal to more of them. It would be a broader topic. Something they could learn and apply to their everyday lives."

She nodded in agreement, completely unaware of the internal battle going on in me. Imagine a student setting up an altar in class! Tiffany smiled and thoughtfully added, "Thank you. I'll do that." Meanwhile, I sighed in relief. My discomfort had not shown. Thankfully, Tiffany walked away and on her speech day did a wonderful presentation on art deco with a ten-page outline attached.

Several weeks later, a visibly shaken Tiffany entered the classroom, her hair disheveled and her countenance anxious. We spoke after class. "Professor Joy," she said still reeling from her experience, "my boyfriend beat me up badly." She paused for a breath. "It was the last thing I expected. I saw a counselor, and they have me on medication. I talked with my mom, and she is helping me out tremendously."

I listened as she poured out her story. Then we hugged and wept together. "I am so sorry," I offered. We continued to talk after class. She felt comfortable confiding some of the details of her struggle—and I know that it was because God had given a ready answer when I needed it most.

> My voice rises to God, and I will cry aloud; My voice rises to God, and He will hear me.
>
> —Ps. 77:1

> Call to Me and I will answer you, and I will tell you great and mighty things, which you do not know.
>
> —Jer. 33:3

An Extraordinary Surprise

Each semester, students in my speech classes do a live demonstration before the class. They are encouraged to be creative and utilize as many visual aids at their disposal for a powerful presentation. Claire, a petite young lady in her early twenties, approached me just before class began. She wore a sleeveless, trendy blouse that allowed me to see the elaborate tattoos that covered both of her arms almost completely. It was odd, because it did not seem to match her personality at all, as she was such a bright and cheerful girl.

"Professor Joy," she started, "you said to pick a topic we were passionate about for the next speech and well...I would like to show the class how to assemble a snake habitat." Taking in my Indiana Jones' "I hate snakes" expression, she quickly added, "But don't worry; I won't bring the snake. I just would love to teach the class about how to take care of one."

With this, I was appeased, and we parted company in good spirits. That is until the day of her speech arrived. As I approached the door to the classroom, an excited Claire waited for me with a strange-looking burlap sack at her feet. "Professor Joy," she exclaimed. "I know I originally wasn't going to bring the snake, but...you said we would get extra credit if we had more visual aids...so, I brought Freddy. He's in the sack," she said gesturing to her feet. "I don't have to take him out if you don't want me to."

I pondered the situation for a moment and prayed. Claire was gazing at me with those hopeful eyes. I looked down at the sack. It was a small one; it could not have held anything much bigger than a grass snake. The aquarium that housed it was not much bigger than the sack. I looked back at Claire who was waiting expectantly.

"All right, here's what we'll do, Claire. Ask the class how they feel about it, and if enough of them are comfortable with it, then you can take the snake out."

"Yes!' she shouted and hurried inside.

When it was Claire's turn to speak, she politely told the class her dilemma. They immediately agreed to her idea. The male students were especially impressed with "snake girl." Meanwhile, I stood at the door ready to answer any questions, if need be, that security might have.

All went well until near the end of her presentation, Claire pulled out a nine-foot boa constrictor from her tiny sac! Suddenly the first three rows were standing by me in the doorway! Claire continued with her presentation nonchalantly with the snake wrapped around her body and draped over her tattooed arms. All the while, I found myself praying, "Dear Jesus, please protect her. Don't let it hurt her." However, I needn't have worried; she was fine. Sometimes God surprises me with His fun sense of humor! He affirmed Claire, protected all of us, and made it memorable. He can take an ordinary day and make it extraordinary. I will never forget that day!

You will make known to me the path of life; in Your **presence** is fullness of **joy**; in Your right hand there are pleasures forever.

—Ps. 16:11

Chapter 14

Beauty for Ashes

For He himself is our peace.

—Eph. 2:14

BROKEN BY BETRAYAL

HE WAS EIGHTEEN when I first met him. Sun-streaked hair and a crooked smile, he was a surfer but with a slight build. I'll never forget his last name; it had the ring of nobility or wealth attached to it. He sat in the back of the class, but you always felt there was another place he would rather be. His infectious smile was self-assured and confident. The popular mischievous kids had surrounded him in that back row.

As a new teacher, I was somewhat caught off guard by this kind of attitude. Quite frankly, it was at times intimidating. Being so young, I was still battling my own insecurities. "What do they think about me—the way I dress and act?" "Will they see the light of Christ radiating from within me?" "How can I introduce Christ to them within the context of this class?" "Will I ever get to share this?" I prayed for God to give me the courage I needed to share with students not much younger than I was.

Overall, Phillip was a respectful kid. Just once, I caught him daydreaming in class. He apologized, saying that he had other things on his mind at that. This was springtime, and the students were anxiously awaiting summer. The cold blustery weather of winter had passed and the beauty of the new season was upon us. Phillip was excited to begin teaching surfing at a summer camp where he would mentor the kids. In spite of his outwardly confident demeanor, he had a great heart of compassion and patience toward children. He talked endlessly of how much he enjoyed this, what a wonderful family he had, and about his girlfriend.

As class wrapped up and we said our good-byes, the students raced off into the blissful sunrise of summer. They were eager to see friends and family and enjoy their vacation time. I watched them leave. I never expected to see Phillip again. I was teaching a general education course, required for all majors, and I doubted if Phillip's business major would require another communication class.

It had been a fun class, and I had enjoyed teaching it. Interpersonal Communication, at its heart, afforded us opportunities to integrate Christian principles into the coursework. My mandate was that if we communicated better, we would love each other better.

Much to my surprise, I saw Phillip a year later. He said he liked my teaching style and wanted to take another course with me. I was pleasantly surprised. It was the beginning of summer. This was a short course, so soon Phillip would be able to work at his beloved summer camp. Several weeks into the course, however, Phillip disappeared. No one knew what might have happened to him. I waited, watched, and prayed.

Some days later, as I turned the corner to come into class, I was relieved to see Phillip waiting for me in the back of the classroom. He immediately approached me, apologizing fiercely. With all of his hours working with the kids during previous summers and with all his surfing, he had been diagnosed with skin cancer on his chest. To drive home the point that he was being honest, and had not been skipping class, Phillip raised his shirt to show me that the doctors had removed his nipples! I believed him. I remember smiling to myself after class thinking, "He was so sincere, but a doctor's note would have been fine."

As the weeks wore on, news came that Phillip would need to stay out of the sun that summer. He was grieved that he would not be able to help, but always mentioned that his family was encouraging him and that things would be better next summer.

I didn't see Phillip again for two more weeks. Then, one day, in the beginning of class, a tear-stained and broken Phillip popped his head in the door. "Could I speak with you?" he said making no eye contact. I could sense this was an emergency. I released the class to do some group work so we could freely talk. Sitting outside the classroom, he began to pour out his story.

He had been at a party. As he entered into his friend's house, he began to search through the rooms looking for his girlfriend of seven months. He had found her in the arms of another man in the very act. Stunned and slightly numb, he had left as this new boyfriend began shouting profanities at him. Sadly, his girlfriend was also vocal about renouncing his claim to her. He had loved her, he said. This was the second time this had happened to him.

I listened as another tear rolled down his face. He wouldn't be able to teach summer camp that summer. His body, although free of the cancer, bore the scars. He was clearly depressed. I reached out to him, offered to pray with him, and offered to get him help. We made arrangements for him to meet with a few of our young people immediately. I asked him about counseling. Finally, I was able to share with him about a loving Father who had sent His Son to die for him, and I got to share a little of my testimony.

He listened politely, but his lip remained stiff. He said, without anger, that he didn't believe in God. "I have a loving family," he said. "We'll get through this." Then, I watched him step onto the elevator, so despondent, so hopeless. I never saw him again.

One day on my way across campus at the end of the day, I ran across a former student of mine who had been in that class. He recognized me and asked how I was doing. I told him I was exuberant after a fruitful day of teaching. We chitchatted a bit before he suddenly asked, "Did you hear what happened to Phillip?" "No," I replied. "Not since last summer. How is he doing?" He added abruptly and without emotion, "He killed himself."

I was stunned. My face fell. I could barely speak. My former student stammered, "I'm sorry to ruin your day," and he started to make a hasty exit. "When?" I managed to ask before he left. "Last summer sometime," he replied. Phillip had missed his appointment with our friends from church. He had never connected with them.

I walked home in a fog, crying out to God for answers. He was gone. Phillip was gone. Rotting in the ground somewhere was a healthy nineteen-year-old. Gone! "Oh, God!" It was too late to tell him of the majesty of Christ. He knew now, but gone was the chance for salvation. I cried, "Could I have done more?" Phillip's family was crushed by the tragedy. They were atheists. How do you explain to parents that your son is eternally separated from God—forever?

Then, in the midst of my troubles, I heard that still, small voice. "You tried, Joy. You shared with him My heart, and he refused." God gently comforted me. "He refused."

The guilt and condemnation washed away. That week I felt a new awakening...a new beginning. There was a new sense of urgency to share with others because we may never have another chance. We need a holy boldness to confess the gospel before others without fear of condemnation.

Phillip's life is a fragrance to me, an encouragement to share with others. He was a youth made in God's image whom God deeply cherished. Jesus died for Phillip, yet he refused the gift of grace. Phillip was an amazing young man—and his legacy in my life? It is that others should know the truth and that the truth should set them free. I pray that his story will encourage you to learn the truth that will set you free. If so, then it is a seed.

> I am still confident of this: I will see the goodness of the Lord in the land of the living.
>
> —Ps. 27:13 NIV

A Word in Season

> Circumstances may appear to wreck our lives and God's plans, but God is not helpless among the ruins. God's love is still working. He comes in and takes the calamity and uses it victoriously, working out His wonderful plan of love.
>
> —Eric Liddell

With iron-gray hair swept back into a loosely coiled bun, she stood and leaned over me to show me something on the computer. Her name was

Gayle, and she was my trainer for a temp job at a call center that I took between jobs after graduate school. Stooped over, wearing baggy clothes to hide her tired frame, Gayle showed me the ropes of data entry.

Since this was a call center, I was confined to a cubicle and a headset for eight long hours a day with exactly two fifteen-minute breaks and a half-hour lunch. We were always flooded with calls regarding credit checks and mobile set-ups, and so I was thankful for even a brief respite. The monotony of the job could at times be grueling. Fortunately, I had a kind boss, who did not mind if I was a minute or two late in returning to work.

Gayle and I chatted during my first two days of work as she trained me personally. While we worked side by side, I felt led to share the story of Joseph. She listened graciously as I retold the story of Joseph in Egypt—how Potiphar's wife had betrayed him, and how he later ended up in prison. "He had not done anything to be placed in that prison," I said. "In fact, he had been acting righteously, but God saw him and comforted him. And Joseph learned to forgive those who had hurt him."

Soon, he was made the head over the prison, and later, when he was released, Joseph was placed second in command over all Egypt. God placed him in a position to help his brothers, for he stewarded the grain and storehouses at a time when famine struck," I finished.

Gayle had listened quietly to the story, and then we went back to work. As the afternoon turned into early evening, I packed up and went home unaware that anything I had shared had stirred her. Driving off, I glimpsed the sunset in my rear view window, and smiled thinking about the day and the restful evening ahead of me.

The next day at work, Gayle surprised me. Mild-mannered, but very matter-of-fact, she began. "I went home and read that story about Joseph," she said quietly. "You know, the one you were telling me about yesterday?" I nodded my head in response. I was shocked.

Slowly, Gayle began to open up. "You see, I used to work in food services," she said. "I worked hard and did the best I could. But one day I was fired for something that was not my fault." She paused and her eyes met mine. "And I have been *here* ever since." Looking around, she shared, "Sometimes I feel like that Joseph in prison."

I nodded my head. I could understand how Gayle could view our routine as a prison. Gayle and I continued to talk over lunch and we prayed together. I was thankful for this opportunity, for it would be two months before I would see her again.

Then one day, something amazing occurred. Had I not "happened" to pop my head out of my cubicle at that moment, I might not have heard Gayle's parting remarks as she prepared to resign her post and say her good-byes to several other staff workers.

Gayle was talking with a light in her eyes that I had never seen before. She glanced over and saw me in my cubicle. Smiling, she said, "Joy doesn't know this," she paused, "but I am going back to school." My eyes met hers and mine suddenly moistened with tears. Softly she said, "I would like to open my own catering business."

I will never forget the look on her face or the smile that crossed it. I sat down in my cubicle and cried silently, thanking God for this small answer to prayer. God had taken a woman beaten down by circumstances and given her hope. Several weeks later, I, too, found a more permanent job. But I will never forget the small bunch of fruit from that one. Had I not popped my head up at that instant, I might never have known. But God wanted me to know that my labor had not been in vain. Through those months, God had provided bread for my table, but I think He was more interested in providing real bread to one who needed Him more. Jesus comes to set the captives free. He sends us to help those who have lost hope, so that they may be released from prison.

> To proclaim liberty to captives and freedom to prisoners; to proclaim the favorable year of the LORD.
>
> —Isa. 61:1-2

> "Stephen, full of grace and power, was performing great wonders and signs among the people."
>
> —Acts 6:8

Chosen to be one of the lucky seven who were honored along with Phillip to serve at widows' tables, Stephen would see God magnified in his life with a most glorious ending while he was preaching the Word. The authorities had brought Stephen in on trumped up charges, bringing in false witnesses stating that, "This man incessantly speaks against this holy place and the Law; for we have heard him say that this Nazarene, Jesus, will destroy this place and alter the customs which Moses handed down to us" (Acts 6:13-14). Stephen refuted each one of the charges, rebuking the men for their unwillingness to accept their true Messiah.

Stephen's face glowed like an angel's as he gave testimony of God's faithfulness by recounting the marvelous works and covenant promises of the One they called Yahweh. (Acts 6:15) As he elaborated on God's provision in Egypt, the wilderness, and eventually the Promised Land, the freedmen, Cyrenians and Alexandrians, listened with anger. Stephen gave glory to God for keeping His promise to Abraham, Isaac, and Jacob and those who came after them. He recalled God's assurance to Abraham—to give the Promised Land to him and his descendents as a possession (see Acts 7:5). This was promised even though Abraham did not have a son or land on which to live at the time!

> By faith, Abraham, when he was called, obeyed by going out to a place which he was to receive an inheritance; and he went out, not knowing where he was going…for he was looking for the city which has foundations, whose architect and builder is God.
>
> —Heb. 11:8,10

By faith Abraham left his country and relatives, to "come into the land that I will show you" (Acts 7:3). What Abraham did may not have made sense in the natural, but then, we are dealing with the God of the supernatural.

Stephen continued to recount the lives of Abraham, Joseph, Moses, and David while the people listened. It was not until Stephen addressed the crowd's rejection of Jesus as Messiah that they became angry. Yet, gazing into Heaven he was rewarded with quite a picture.

> But being full of the Holy Spirit, he gazed intently into heaven and saw the glory of God, and Jesus standing at the right hand of God; and he said, "Behold, I see the heavens opened up and the Son of Man **standing** at the right hand of God."
>
> —Acts 7:55-56

According to *The New John Gill Exposition of the Entire Bible*, Stephen's words also affirm his innocence as he references Jesus as the "Son of Man."

> He calls Jesus "the son of man"; a name by which he often called himself in his state of humiliation; and that though he was now glorified, it being the name of the Messiah in (Psalms 80:17; Daniel 7:13) as was well known to the Jews; and this Stephen said to show that God was on his side, and to let them know what honor was done him, what divine supports and comforts he had, and that he was an eyewitness of Jesus, and of his being alive, and in glory.[44]

But not only this, Jesus is standing at the right hand of the Father! Mike Bickle also speaks about this honor given to Stephen. Jesus is not seated; He is standing to receive Stephen. Scripture affirms this; these are Jesus' words while being questioned regarding his position beside the Father.

They asked Him to admit whether or not He was the Christ. Here is Jesus' answer, "'If I tell you, you will not believe; and if I ask a question, you will not answer. But from now on **the Son of Man will be seated at the right hand** of the power **of God**.' And they all said, 'Are You the Son of God, then?' And He said to them, 'Yes, I am'" (Luke 22:67-70).

At Stephen's words, the men rebelled, and "cried out with a loud voice, and covered their ears and rushed at him with one impulse. ...When they had driven him out of the city, they began stoning him" (Acts 7:57-58). Stephen's last words in his final moments of life echo Jesus' words. "'Lord Jesus, receive my spirit!' Then falling to his knees, he cried out in a loud voice, 'Lord, do not hold this sin against them!' Having said this, he fell asleep" (Acts 7:59-60).

A WORTHY FOLLOWER

By his martyrdom, Stephen, a disciple/follower of Christ, echoes the very actions of Christ as He approached the cross.

> When they came to the place called The Skull, there they crucified Him and the criminals, one on the right and the other on the left.

But Jesus was saying, "Father, forgive them; for they do not know what they are doing." And they cast lots, dividing up His garments among themselves.

—Luke 23:33-34

Like Christ, Stephen also forgave his captors, for he saw the greater implications of their sin and did not wish them to receive the judgment they might deserve in an earthly court. "Do not fear those who kill the body but are unable to kill the soul; but rather fear Him who is able to destroy both soul and body in hell" (Matt. 10:28).

> Stephen fixed his eyes on heaven and beheld the glory of God.

For we must appear before the judgment seat of Christ, so that each one may be recompensed for his deeds in the body, according to what he has done, whether good or bad.

—2 Cor. 5:10

Chapter 15

Called by Name

Leave the broken, irreversible past in God's hands, and step out into the invincible future with Him.

—Oswald Chambers

FISHERS OF MEN

IN THE BEGINNING, they called him Simon, the one who leans. Later Jesus renamed him Peter, or *petra*, which means "the rock."[45] Peter, a fisherman by trade, had dropped his nets to follow after the One they called Yeshua, or Jesus. He had witnessed His many miracles, seen the incredible healings, and been privileged to sit in the company of eleven others for the Last Supper (see John 13). Jesus had also washed Peter's feet before the meal despite his initial protest.

Peter had been the first among the disciples to call Jesus the Christ, the Son of God (Matt. 16:16). He had been sent out with the other disciples in Jesus' name and later witnessed the Transfiguration (see Luke 9:28-36). He had waited with Jesus in Garden of Gethsemane, observed Judas's betrayal, and sliced off an officer's ear in protest at the ensuing arrest (Luke 22). Thankfully, for the soldier, it was an ear that

> Jesus is the Christ,
> the risen Lord.

Jesus later healed before He was taken to the authorities. Jesus was being obedient to the will of the Father, and in doing so fulfilled the promises and prophecies of centuries before.

And then the heartbreak...Peter's betrayal. Before the cock crowed three times on the eve of Jesus' arrest, Peter denied knowing Christ. Yet God was not surprised. Jesus even spoke these words ahead of time to Peter for He knew they would come to pass:

> Simon, Simon, behold, Satan has demanded permission to sift you like wheat; but I have prayed for you, that your faith may not fail; and you, when once you have turned again, strengthen your brothers.
> —Luke 22:31-32

Peter initially protested. "Lord, with You, I am ready to go both to prison and to death!" (Luke 22:33). But Jesus knew the truth; He sees the end from the beginning. He knew Peter would deny Him, but He also prayed for Peter's restoration. Amidst all the commotion, the gathering of the Sanhedrin, and the presence of the Roman guard, Jesus was at peace. He was going to make all things new.

> For the joy set before Him, He endured the cross.
> —Heb. 12:2

SIFTED LIKE WHEAT

Meanwhile, Peter was indeed sifted as Christ lovingly warned him he would be. Before the cock crowed three times that day, Peter denied being a disciple of Jesus to a servant girl and several others. Imagine Peter's heartbreak as he heard the rooster crow later that day. Scripture tells us that, "He went out and wept bitterly" upon remembering what Jesus had told him earlier that day (Luke 22:62).

I recall a powerful scene from *The Passion of the Christ* directed by Mel Gibson where we see Peter confronted with a bleeding and disheveled Jesus. His eyes meet His beloved Savior's, and he is struck with how deeply he has betrayed Jesus. Peter later encounters Jesus' mother and James in the corridor only to begin weeping inconsolably. He does not wish to be touched; he feels so ashamed and unworthy.

Now fast forward. Jesus was crucified, died, and was buried. Yet on the third day, He rose again in accordance with the Scriptures. Where is Peter after all of this has taken place? Surprisingly, he has gone back to his old profession—fishing. After a long night on the boat without catching anything, Peter and several other disciples may have been weary. When Jesus sees them, He begins to reach out to Peter in restoration.

> So Jesus said to them, "Children, you do not have any fish, do you?" They answered Him, "No." And He said to them, "Cast the net on the right-hand side of the boat and you will find a catch."
> —John 21:5-6

They did as they were told, and the catch was so great they could not haul in the nets. And this after a full night of fishing and catching nothing! John recognized Jesus first saying, "It is the Lord" (John 21:7). Imagine what it must have felt like to see the Lord before your very eyes when you had seen him crucified only days earlier.

> So when Simon Peter heard that it was the Lord, he put his outer garment on (for he was stripped for work), and **threw himself into the sea.**
> —John 21:7

Peter could hardly contain himself. He was not going to wait until he reached the shore at a slower pace; he dove in! The boat was approximately one-hundred feet from shore when Peter leapt into the water. The other disciples followed in the boat and brought it and the net full of fish to the dock.

Now the disciples gazed with awe and wonder upon the One who had been pierced. Their friend was standing before them alive and filled with the love of God. And He had come to dine with them once again. This time it would be different. It was morning, and they were about to enjoy breakfast together.

> Weeping may last for the night, but a shout of joy comes in the morning.
> —Ps. 30:5

Jesus begins with a simple question of restoration. "Simon, son of John, do you love Me more than these?" Peter replies, "Yes, Lord; You know that I love You." And then Jesus responds saying, "Tend My lambs." (John 21:15) But Jesus does not stop there. He asks the question twice more.

> He said to him again a second time, "Simon, son of John, do you love Me?" He said to Him, "Yes, Lord; You know that I love You." He said to him, "Shepherd My sheep." He said to him the third time, "Simon, son of John, do you love Me?" Peter was grieved because He said to Him the third time, "Do you love Me?" And he said to Him, "Lord, You know all things; You know that I love You." Jesus said to him, "Tend My sheep."
>
> —John 21:16-17

With each question, Jesus is erasing the past, and all condemnation Peter must have felt in denying Him. For each denial, Peter gives an affirmation of truth. And after each answer, Jesus gives him a loving request. Remember? Jesus prayed for Peter that when he returned to Him, he would strengthen his brothers (see Luke 22:31-32). This battle would not end in defeat, but rather in a destiny restored as God beheld his beloved Peter.

Peter goes on to wait for the coming of the Holy Spirit at Pentecost. When he is empowered with the Holy Spirit, He goes on to preach a fiery sermon and sees 3,000 converts in one day! And that is just the beginning. What Jesus said earlier has come to pass. "I also say to you that you are **Peter**, and upon this **rock** I will build My church; and the gates of Hades will not overpower it" (Matt. 16:18). Peter would go on to fulfill his calling, and later be crucified upside down so as not to take any glory from Jesus' death and resurrection.

> He who began a good work in you will perfect it until the day of Christ Jesus.
>
> —Phil. 1:6

Chapter 16

Her Name Is "Joy"

You will make known to me the path of life; in Your presence is fullness of **joy**; in Your right hand there are pleasures forever.

—Ps. 16:11

BITTER TO JOYFUL

LIKE PETER, ANOTHER young one was about to be restored and have her story written into God's countless chapters of redemption. For many often think of the term "Mara" referring to the waters of Marah, which the Israelites journeyed to as they made their way through the wilderness. In Exodus 15:23, we read that, "When they came to Marah, they could not drink the waters of Marah, for they were bitter; therefore it was named Marah." The Lord then instructed them to throw a specific tree into the water, so that it became sweet.

My mother, not realizing the significance of this passage, named me "Mara" because her favorite childhood character bore that name. Unfortunately, in Hebrew, the name "Mara" translates into "bitter" or "bitter waters." The name perfectly described the maiden in Eloise Jarvis McGraw's book, *Mara, Daughter of the Nile*, who was indeed bitter and proud.

As a child, I was never too concerned about the meaning of my name, but I was often frustrated by the way it was mispronounced. An unusual name, most teachers assumed it as "Laura," " Maria," "Maya," " Maria." Calling me "Maria" was very humorous to me, because I am full-blooded Scandinavian, and thus, my blonde hair should have been the giveaway. At least "Laura," which means "victorious one," brought a measure of comfort.

As I grew older and attended seminary, I learned the full implications of my name. I will never forget introducing myself to several divinity students. After shaking hands with them, I watched as their faces masked a look of confusion. "Mara," one repeated thought-fully, "but that does not fit you at all!" I had to laugh, because he was right.

Until I received Jesus as Lord of my life, I had a great deal of bitterness with which to deal. My own poor choices had left me scarred and wounded. However, the Lord, in His Sovereignty, took all those circumstances and situations and changed me.

He was the tree that fell into the waters of Marah. Jesus made the bitter waters sweet.

Amazing Loyalty

> Myrrh is a bitter herb...Yet, myrrh, when it is crushed and burned, releases a sweet aroma before the Lord.
>
> —Dr. Mara Crabtree

My story parallels the story of God's redemption in the Book of Ruth. It begins where Naomi, who has lost her husband and both of her sons, laments over her misfortune. "Do not call me Naomi; call me **Mara**, for the Almighty has dealt very bitterly with me" (Ruth 1:20).

Naomi and her husband had left Bethlehem, which means "house of bread" to travel to Moab during a time of famine.[46] Looking upon her two daughters-in-law to whom she can give no more sons for marriage, Naomi decides to return to Israel seeking a kinsman redeemer. In a famous passage, Ruth, one of her foreign daughters-in-law, decides to come too.

> But Ruth said, "Do not urge me to leave you or turn back from following you; for where you go, I will go, and where you lodge, I will lodge. Your people shall be my people, and your God, my God. Where you die, I will die, and there I will be buried."
>
> —Ruth 1:16-17

Through a miraculous set of circumstances, Ruth eventually marries another relative of Naomi's and bears him a son. Interestingly enough, this son is the grandfather of one of the greatest kings to rule Israel, David.

> So Boaz took Ruth, and she became his wife, and he went in to her. And the LORD enabled her to conceive, and she gave birth to a son. Then the women said to Naomi, "Blessed is the LORD who has not left you without a redeemer today, and may his name become famous in Israel. May he also be to you a restorer of life and a sustainer of your old age; for your daughter-in-law, who loves you and is better to you than seven sons, has given birth to him." So they named him Obed. He is the father of Jesse, the father of David.
>
> —Ruth 4:13-15, 17

And further on down the family line, we see that Jesus comes from the line of David.[47] Truly, it is a miraculous story that only God could write on the pages of history. God transformed a tragedy into one of the happiest stories of all.

> Then I will go to the altar of God, to God my exceeding **joy**; and upon the lyre I shall praise You, O God, my God.
>
> —Ps. 43:4

THE NAME CHANGE

> Joy is not the absence of suffering; it is the Presence of the Lord.
> —Dr. George Jefferson

Several years ago, we were on retreat when the Lord spoke to me about my name. It was a lovely day and our small group had gathered at an outdoor cathedral. Heaven and earth were as one in this setting.

The sun shone through the windows in the stone walls, as the wind blew gently overhead lightly mussing my hair. Aside from the beautiful altar and bell tower at the front, nothing else remained of the cathedral save the remnants of a few windows surrounding the pulpit area. Tall stalks of emerald green grass had grown up around the slates of eroded stone as everyone took their seats. I had a joyful time hanging on a rope, ringing the bell in the bell tower, to start the worship portion of the service. Smiling, I took my seat.

In my hand was a large rock that was supposed to signify a burden I had been carrying. For fun, one of my cohorts had gotten creative and encouraged us to glue a pair of eyes to each one of our rocks, giving them a measure of personality. So, now, my rock looked cute.

Ideally, we were asked to take the rocks with us every place we went—even to the shower—to symbolize that we carry those burdens with us wherever we go. Over the course of those few days, the rock began to signify several things in my life that God was dealing with. Yet, I was unaware of what God had planned for that particular day.

As the service drew to a close, our pastor stood before us and unveiled an altar filled with white rocks. On each were the words "new name" written in Hebrew from Revelation 2:17. "To him who overcomes, to him I will give some of the hidden manna, and I will give him a white stone, and a new name written on the stone which no one knows but he who receives it"(Rev. 2:17). Mike Bickle further elaborates on the significance of this stone. "The stone referred to a precious stone (diamond). White (Gr. *leukos*) refers to 'shining and glistening.'"[48] So in eternity, it will be a beautiful, shining, and glistening diamond with my new name written on it!

It was my turn to lay my old rock on the altar, and pick up the new one. I felt warmed by the sun as a slight breeze floated down through the trees, lifting my hair. As I gazed at the luminous, alabaster stone, something unexpected happened. I distinctly heard God speak to my inner man, saying, "I call you Joy."

It had been so sudden. I paused, smiling. As I stepped away, I thought, "So, others call me "Mara," but He calls me "Joy." Radiant at this new word of truth, I sat down speechless and happy.

And that was that. I did not think any more about it until one of my friends mentioned the idea of changing my name. "Your name does not suit you," he said. "Would you ever consider changing it?" After pondering and praying about this, I invited close friends to give insight as to what I should be called. The responses I received were varied: everything from Rebekah to Guinevere. At the time I thought to keep "Joy" as a middle name since changing one's name must take considerable time and effort. Soon I discovered it was not a huge problem or process! For thirty-four dollars and a week's wait, one can easily change a name.

Back to the drawing board, I opened up the Scriptures to see what God had to say on the subject of name changes. It was there that I found some surprising things. God changed "Simon" from the "the one who leans" to "Peter" which means "the rock." He changed "Saul" to "Paul," "Abram to Abraham;" "Sarai" to "Sarah" to name a few.

> Simon was renamed Peter to speak of his character and position as the rock. Abram's name was changed to Abraham to indicate that he was to be the father of a multitude (Gen. 17:5-15). God changed Sarah's name. Jacob's name was changed to Israel to speak of his place of government and access to God.[49]

God had given them new names—each with a new meaning to glorify what He had done in their lives. *From "bitter" to "joy." What a beautiful transformation that would be,* I thought. In heaven, God would give each of us a new name. "I just got mine early," I laughed.

After speaking with family members, and getting mixed results, I prayerfully went ahead and legally changed my name. As I was leaving the courthouse, I asked the Lord, "Why was this so important? Why are we doing this?" The Lord showed me a picture of Him standing in the mountains. Quietly, He said, "We are taking back the high places."

I pondered that. In ancient Israel's days, there had been many kings; some had honored God while others had been very evil. One of the persistent themes in the Book of Kings is that even though the people still loved and worshipped God, the high places were not taken away. In 1 Kings 14:23, we read, "For they also built for themselves **high places** and sacred pillars and Asherim on every high hill and beneath every luxuriant tree."

In this context, a "high place" signified a place where idolatrous worship was taking place. For again:

> He [the king] did what was right in the sight of the LORD; he did according to all that his father Uzziah had done. Only the high places were not taken away; the people still sacrificed and burned incense on the high places. He built the upper gate of the house of the LORD.
> —2 Kings 15:34-35

In many of these cases, the kings had torn down any false worship in the temple, but failed to remove false worship from the mountains or high places. The Israelites had integrated Baal worship or "Asherim," which was a Babylonian (Astarte)-Canaanite goddess (of fortune and happiness) who was associated with Baal.[50] Thus, the high places are important for many reasons.

BREAKING THE CHAINS

Although a number of my family members have given their lives to Christ, there was still a spirit of unforgiveness that had pervaded previous generations. For instance, my grandmother and her siblings decided one day that they were not going speak to each other ever again. Considering the fact that my grandmother was in her eighties at the time, the chances of reconciliation on this earth were slim. I thought, *How ridiculous!*

New in the faith, I was bold to sit down with my grandmother and explain with the Scriptures why this was wrong. We prayed quietly together, and after several months of intercession, the family was speaking again. My grandmother passed away a short time later. Now, imagine if they had not ever spoken!

The Lord was breaking off this spirit of divisiveness in our family. He showed me that the spirit had grieved His heart long enough, and He was breaking it off me. This would be a new beginning.

Ironically, only my immediate family struggled with my name change. All close friends and acquaintances immediately took to calling me "Joy." Most found it easy to remember. "It just suits you," they would smile. In fact, while attending an outdoor gathering, a dear friend went ahead, alerting about sixty other people to call me "Joy" when they first saw me that evening. It was truly a delight!

MOURNING TO JOY

Now one of the greatest compliments I ever received occurred when I introduced myself. "I am Joy," I said cheerfully. "My, that is perfect!" they remarked, "Joy. Your parents must have known what they were doing when they picked out your name." We smiled at each other, and then I replied, "Yes, indeed, my Father knew exactly what He was doing."

> Then those who sing as well as those who play the flutes shall say, "All my springs of **joy** are in you."
>
> —Ps. 87:7

Chapter 17

The Apple of His Eye

This is the message we have heard from Him and announce to you,
that God is Light, and in Him there is no darkness at all.

—1 John 1:5

THE FATHER'S HEART

DANA WAS A perky, twenty-nine-year-old returning student. She
always presented her material well, and today was no exception. Not only
did she incorporate dynamic video clips and organize her information
well, she delivered her speech in a polished and professional manner.
It was clear that she had put a lot of time and effort into this project.
Needless to say, she exceeded all of my expectations.

When she had finished, the rest of the presenters sheepishly looked
around the room. "Who is next?" I asked offhandedly, still grading her
assignment. Anthony, a curly-haired young man in the front row, gave a
quick response. "That's a tough act to follow, Professor!" We all laughed.
Needless to say, no one wanted to go right away; she had blown the
other students out of the water with her presentation.

Several speeches followed, and I sighed contentedly. It had been
a good day. I was proud of their work. They were learning something
valuable from the material and from each other. As students began to
file out of the classroom, Jeremy, a student who had fallen behind in

his homework, approached me. We worked out a schedule for him to complete his assignments, and I gathered my things to leave for the day.

Surprisingly, Dana had stayed behind as well. Timidly, she approached me. "Professor, how do you think I did?" she asked nervously. Without a second thought, I plunged, "Outstanding! One of the best presentations in the class!"

Dana hesitantly inquired, "Do you think I will receive an "A" for it?" She glanced up at me, uncertain. I smiled. "An A plus, Dana. It was one of the best presentations I have ever seen." Although Dana seemed relieved, she still persisted. "Is there any extra credit I could do to bring my overall grade up?"

I stopped what I was doing. Staring at her dumbfounded, I began, "Dana, you have the highest grade in the class. You have worked hard and deserve your reward. If you do not have a ninety–nine or one hundred as a final grade for the semester, I will be shocked." Meanwhile, Jeremy, who had overheard this conversation, chimed in, "Dude, girl. Your last presentation rocked." He laughed, adding, "I am the one who needs extra credit, not you!"

Dana relaxed a bit more after hearing this. "It's just that...I want my dad to be proud of me." She paused, "I dropped out of school last time because I got pregnant and well...don't get me wrong; I have a beautiful nine-year-old daughter. I just want my dad to be proud of me." Our eyes met. I nodded, understanding.

When she left, Jeremy and I stared at each other. "Dr. Joy," he began, "Why was she so worried? She didn't need to worry."

"I know, Jeremy." I paused, still gazing at Dana's retreating figure, "She is just searching for a father's love." Then turning to him I added, "She does not know she already has it."

The Gift of Mercy

In my early years as a new believer, I recall that I felt a need to repay God for what He had done, to repay Christ for His precious gift. Even though I loved the Lord with my heart, I still felt unworthy. I knew Jesus loved me, but I imagined God the Father was terribly upset. "I guess I have to let her into Paradise," I imagined Him muttering, "but it is only because of You, Jesus."

I loved Jesus for His gift of love to me, and I greatly feared the Father. What I failed to realize was the truth of John 3:16. "For God so loved the world, that He gave His only begotten Son, that whoever believes in Him shall not perish, but have eternal life."

Did you miss that first part too? Let me say it again. "For God so loved the world.... Two very powerful words. *"For God..."* God loved the world. He sent His Son to redeem us from the Fall.

If you have seen Mel Gibson's *The Passion of the Christ*, you might recall the scene just after Christ died on the cross. A single teardrop or raindrop fell from the sky, symbolizing God's deep sorrow as He watched His Son suffer and die on that cross. It was the Father's tear. His love had compelled Christ to the cross.

MADE FOR LOVE

> For I am convinced that neither death, nor life, nor angels, nor principalities, nor things present, nor things to come, nor powers, nor height, nor depth, nor any other created thing, will be able to separate us from the love of God, which is in Christ Jesus our Lord.
> —Rom. 8:38-39

When we encounter God in the place of prayer, we begin to have a revelation of His true character and His divine, yet compassionate, nature. Often in our brokenness, we imagine God to be like our earthly father, and as such we project an image of our own father onto Him. Thus, if our father was dismissive, angry, impatient, or hands off in the way he raised us, there is a tendency to superimpose that image onto God. Yet, nothing could be further from the truth.

God is not the watchmaker who wound up the universe, got it ticking, and then left it alone. He is not distant. God is personal and He has revealed Himself to His people. What's utterly shocking is that in the midst of an extravagant universe that glorifies the wonder and splendor of His majesty, God delights in each and every one of us. He actually takes joy in us. Zephaniah 3:14-17 further proves this point.

Shout for joy, O daughter of Zion! Shout in triumph, O Israel!
Rejoice and exult with all your heart, O daughter of Jerusalem!
The LORD has taken away His judgments against you,
He has cleared away your enemies.
The King of Israel, the LORD, is in your midst;
You will fear disaster no more.
In that day it will be said to Jerusalem: "Do not be afraid, O Zion;
Do not let your hands fall limp. The LORD your God is in your midst,
A victorious warrior. He will exult over you with joy,
He will be quiet in His love, He will rejoice over you with shouts of joy."

A personal breakthrough for me came upon reading Mike Bickle's *Passion for Jesus* where he mentions the fact that God is glad when He gazes upon us. According to Bickle, He is "…a God I didn't have to strive to make happy, because He'd been happy with me from the second I was born into His family."[51] God is not perpetually mad at us, but glad when He fixes His eyes upon us. Reading that passage caused something in me to shift, thus changing my emotional chemistry.[52] Feelings of condemnation fled; I felt secure in knowing that He loved me deeply despite my flaws. And, as the knowledge of His love flowed into me, His love flowed out naturally as well.

LONGING FOR LOVE

Many in this generation are giving themselves away into the embraces of others who cannot provide what they need most: the security of knowing that they are loved.

The United States leads the world in fatherless families with roughly 24 million children (or 34 percent of all kids in the United States) living in homes where the father does not reside. Nearly 40 percent of children in father-absent homes have not seen their dad during the past year, and more than half of all fatherless children have never been in their dad's home. The number of children being raised by single mothers has more than tripled between 1960 and 2000.[53]

Thus, the impact of not having a father figure can be equally devastating for a child. Adolescents with a negative relationship with their fathers reported increased drug and alcohol abuse as well.[54] Why? Perhaps the pain they feel over the loss or absence of a father leads them to find something to ease that pain.

Even for the very best of fathers, there is still human failing. Only God is the perfect parent; the rest of us are simply trying. I would highly recommend Mike Bickle's *Passion for Jesus* for more information on this subject. Other resources that relate to this subject include: *Total Forgiveness* by R.T. Kendall and *Heart Forgiveness* by James Jordan. It can be the beginning of a journey to discovering what a treasure you really are to God, and the start of deep and lasting healing from the past.

HEALING THE WOUNDED SPIRIT

In my life, I have come across several resources that expedite the healing process by addressing the foundational roots of many of the sins in our lives and those of our ancestors. Often, it is not so much what has happened to us, but rather what we believe about it. Asking Jesus to remove the pain and legal ground for these hurts prevents the enemy from sowing any lies that would cripple us later in life. Exploring the generational curses, ungodly beliefs associated with these, and soul/spirit hurts helps us to see a true picture of why we feel the way we do. For further exploration of this subject, I *highly* recommend *Restoring the Foundations* by Chester and Betsy Kylstra.

In terms of addressing how our parents initially felt about us before we were born, I recently discovered *The Ancient Paths Seminar and Handbook*, which outlines this in detail. "Were we wanted?" "What were the conditions surrounding our birth?" and "How has this impacted our perception of self?" In exploring this topic with the Lord, it is important to remember that God loves us, and He is healer. According to John and Paula Sanford in *Healing the Wounded Spirit*, we discover that for each of the conditions before the child was born, the following traits generally were observed in the behavior of the children after birth.[55]

If a child is not wanted	Striving, performance, inordinate desire to please, (Or the opposite, rejecting before he can be rejected), tension, apologizing, frequent illness, problems with bonding
Conceived out of wedlock	Having a deep sense of shame, lack of belonging
The parents face a bad time	Believing "I'm a burden" financially or parents are too young, not ready
A child being formed is believed to be one gender but is the other one	Sexual identification problems, sometimes a cause for homosexuality, "I was wrong from the beginning."
Mother has inordinate fear of delivery	Fear, insecurity, fear of childbirth
Mother is afraid of gaining too much weight or does not eat properly	Insatiable hunger, anger
C-Section	Intense craving for all kinds of physical contact

Again, each of these conditions can be addressed, so that God can root out feelings of unforgiveness with our parents or with God, so that we can be free to love and be loved unconditionally.

RECEIVING THE GIFT

Like Dana, who felt she had to make it up to her earthly father for her fall from grace, I attempted to do the same with my heavenly Father. Feeling so unworthy of such great love, of such great sacrifice, I did my best to make amends for the past. I was contending against shame. I could not fathom how a loving God could accept me, forgive me, and set me free without me paying a cent. How could I repay so great a debt?

Then, God did an amazing series of things that set my heart on a journey to understand how much He loved me. At a worship service, I was reminded of the parable of a king returning to settle his accounts.

Matthew 18:23-34 recounts the tale. "When he [the king] had begun to settle them, one who owed him ten thousand talents was brought to him" (Matt. 18:24). Scholars have researched how much a talent would have been worth. One source states that,

> A talent was a sum of money, or *weight* of silver or gold, amounting to three thousand shekels. A silver *shekel* was worth, after the captivity, not far from half a dollar of our money. A talent of silver was worth 1,519 dollars; of gold, 24,309 dollars…If these were silver talents, as is probable, then the sum owed by the servant was 16,180,000 dollars. The sum is used to show that the debt was immensely large, and that our sins are so great that they cannot be estimated or numbered.[56]

To put this in perspective, America's national debt is in the trillions of dollars, while the taxes for Galilee and Perea were only *200* talents per annum.[57] Compare this now to the man in Matthew 18 who owed *10,000* talents to the king! The debt was enormous!

> The debt was too large for me to ever repay in my lifetime.

Once the realization of this hit me, I began to see Father God from a different perspective.

CHRISTMAS

Imagine you have a child, and at a great price to yourself personally, you give that child the greatest gift he or she could ever hope to receive. Imagine the love with which the gift is given and the sacrifice involved. You as a parent cannot wait to see your child's joy and thanksgiving at receiving it.

Now, imagine that your child opens the gift. Your eyes expectantly await the cry of joy that will escape their lips for the gift you so longed to give them. They begin unwrapping the bow, peeling off the tape, and then finally they lift off the lid of the box their gift rests in. The moment has at last arrived. You expect them to cheerfully jump up, run into your arms, and give you a great, big hug.

Picture now, instead of being joyful, your beloved child turns to you with a look of shame and downcast eyes. You stare at him in confusion and shock. Then, your child says something you least expect. He murmurs that he wishes to give you money for the gift!

Your mouth hangs open in surprise. The gift you have given him is priceless. It was given in love, and it is not something that could be earned. Repayment would almost be offensive, wouldn't it?

> For by grace you have been saved through faith; and that not of yourselves, **it is** the gift of God; not as a result of works, so that no one may boast.
>
> —Eph. 2:8-9

We are given the gift of His grace and mercy. A gift is translated *charis* in the New Testament Greek, which means a "blessing, concession, credit, favor, gift, grace, gracious, gracious work, gratitude, thank, thankfulness, thanks."[58] It is interesting to me that the definition begins with "blessing, concession, and credit" and ends with "thankfulness and thanks." The implication here is that the latter should be the heart response to the gift given. Meanwhile, the word "works" in the Greek translates as *ergon* which means an "action, behavior, deed, deeds, doing, effectual, labor, result."[59]

Chapter 18

Coming Home

The **Father loves** the Son and has given all things into His hand.
—John 3:35

A TALE OF TWO BROTHERS

THERE ONCE WERE two brothers: one was a prodigal, the other, an elder brother. The prodigal son goes to town spending his father's inheritance on "loose living" until finally he finds himself penniless. Destitute, he contemplates his future. "Will his father forgive him?" When he returns home, he is forgiven and greeted with open arms by his father.

Jesus, in relaying the story, also reinforces the message of the Father's love by first telling the stories of a lost coin and a lost sheep prior to sharing the tale of the prodigal son. What is interesting is a shepherd's examination of this very passage. In his book, *A Shepherd Looks at Psalm 23*, Phillip Keller describes the painstaking process of shepherding and the watchful eye a shepherd must have in caring for his flock. Keller also describes the concern a shepherd has when one of his sheep is missing due to the danger they might be in if they are cast.

> A cast sheep is a very pathetic sight. Lying on its back, its feet in the
> air, it flays away frantically struggling to get up, without success…If

the owner does not arrive on the scene in a reasonably short time, the sheep will die…(predators)…and…As it lies there struggling, gases begin to build up in the rumen. As they expand they tend to cut off blood circulation to extremities of the body, especially the legs.[60]

So, the prodigal son is likened to the sheep in the previous passage. His sin left him feeling muddy from the miry clay, but he was about to be lifted up, forgiven, and unconditionally loved by his father.

But while he was still a long way off, his father saw him and felt compassion for him, and ran and embraced him and kissed him.

—Luke 15:20

This adds new meaning to the passage in Luke when you read Phillip Keller's story of searching for the one lost sheep.

Again and again I would spend hours searching for a single sheep that was missing. Then more often than not, I would see it at a distance, down on its back, lying helpless. At once I would start to run toward it—hurrying as fast as I could—for every minute was critical. Within me was a mingled sense of fear and joy…As soon as I reached the cast ewe my very first impulse was to pick it up.[61]

Are you again starting to feel precious to the Lord? He would leave the ninety-nine in search of you because He loves you and desires that no harm come to you. He races toward you, His beloved, when you least expect it. That is how unconditional His love is.

THE POISON OF ENVY

And this commandment we have from Him, that the one who loves God should love his brother also.

—1 John 4:21

The story of the prodigal son may be familiar to many. But what of the elder brother? Until recently, I never saw the connection as vividly as I do now.

Imagine, if you will, a house. Inside that house is a loving Father. For the purposes of this story, imagine that the house represents the Father's heart.[62] Outside the walls of that house were things that allured the younger brother. He went out from the house in search of love, but he did not find it. Penniless and destitute, he weighed his options. Could he go home again? Would his father welcome him back? He was truly sorry for all that he had done. Finally, the younger brother decides his only option is to return, but he concedes that he would be happy to live as a hired hand, if only he could return home. Much to his surprise, when he does return, his father welcomes him and has a feast to celebrate his return.

Now enter the elder brother. Upon discovering that his brother, who had wasted his father's money, had returned, the elder brother did not celebrate.

> Now his older son was in the field, and when he came and approached the house, he heard music and dancing...And he [the servant] said to him, "Your brother has come, and your father has killed the fattened calf because he has received him back safe and sound." But he [the elder brother] became angry and was not willing to go in; and his father came out pleading with him. But he answered and said to his father, "Look! For so many years I have been serving you and I have never neglected a command of yours; and yet you have never given me a young goat, so that I might celebrate with my friends; but when this son of yours came, who has devoured your wealth with prostitutes, you killed the fattened calf for him."
>
> —Luke 15:25, 27-30

Do you hear the anger, envy, and indignation in his voice? The elder brother stood outside the house, refusing to go in despite the father's beckoning.

I used to think the elder brother was justified, until I realized he too was unwilling to enter into the father's love. He had come from the fields after a full day's work. He was **working** to earn the father's love.[63] What he didn't realize, much as Dana didn't, was that it was love he already had.

Now listen to the father's response. "Son, you have *always* been with me, and all that is mine is yours. But we had to celebrate and rejoice, for this brother of yours was dead and *has begun to live*, and was lost and has been found" (Luke 15:31-32). The elder brother had been found faithful, and yet he did not understand the Father's love. God desires all to be saved. He loves us all. His love is a gift, and it is one we are given because we are His children.

> Beloved, let us love one another, for love is from God; and everyone who loves is born of God and knows God.
>
> —1 John 4:7

ADOPTED

Many of us have what is called an "orphan spirit." For years, I had heard the phrase, but wondered exactly what that meant. One could say that it is: a false belief that we must accomplish everything under our own power because our "Father" will not do this for us.

Many believe that God is somehow disinterested in our affairs and the day-to-day events in our lives. Once again, it's like the watchmaker who winds up the universe, sets it into motion, and then steps back, disinterested. The expression, "God helps those who help themselves," seems to be ingrained in our psyche. But truthfully, that expression is nowhere in the Scriptures. We have a God who covers us...if we will let Him. It is all about receiving His love...receiving from Him. It entails a willingness on our part to allow Him to give us His best. It also involves our surrender.

I once lived in a terrible apartment straight off of an episode of "The Cosby Show." Remember the episode where Sonya and Alvin move into a rundown apartment right after college? Well, although the water in my apartment was not brown, there were many other issues that contributed to my departure some months later.

First of all, the building itself was Pre-World War Two with the same sink, tub, and fixtures from that era. Although this may sound romantic, the place was dusty and was badly in need of a fresh coat of paint. The fact that the wiring was done mostly with extension cords and nothing had been restored since the 40s made it barely livable.

The other tenants below had pets, and so, one was greeted by the occasional plastic bag of dog poop on the front porch, followed by an interior hallway that reeked of urine and dog hair. Rounding the banisters, you could see that the plaster was falling off the walls and the trim. Most trick-or-treaters never made it past the first floor. And then, there was the back staircase...three levels of rotting rust steps awaiting collapse at any given moment. Needless to say, I was not thrilled with the place.

Over the course of my stay, I battled bed bugs, lice, and roaches that could be classified as mammals. I didn't know that they could be so large! I was told never to eat in my room simply because they would emerge from the many painted over cracks we had in the molding. Only once did I indulge in eating pizza in my room, only to discover a roach waiting for me when I returned to the room.

Then, one day everything changed. Lightning struck the sewer vent. God had staged a jailbreak. Within weeks, I needed a new place to live! God had orchestrated this because He had better things in mind for me. I simply had to learn to receive from my Daddy. I no longer needed to live under those conditions.

> Because you are sons, God has sent forth the Spirit of His Son into our hearts, crying, "**Abba**! Father!"
> —Gal. 4:6

WALKING INTO GOD'S PROMISES

While praying, the Lord showed me a picture of the place He had set aside for me. It was everything I had prayed for...down to the last detail. Even the sinks had my favorite type of handle! Within a month, I was living there! Each morning, I awoke in wonder that God had prepared a place for me. I imagined Him smiling, knowing that this was a gift He had longed to give to me. He saw the countless nights I had cried out for respite at the old apartment. He had seen every tear and heard every beat of my heart. He truly desired to release me from prison.

I liken that old rundown apartment to the orphan spirit and the beautiful, new place to the Father's heart. Many of us settle for suffering, thinking that God is always shaping our character as if God *only* desires suffering. Yet, there is a bigger tapestry God is weaving. "What doesn't kill you, makes you stronger," is the mantra of many. And although, "God does work all things for good," and "suffering produces perseverance and perseverance, proven character," there is a bigger picture people often miss. *God loves us.* Let me just say that again, *God loves His children.* And like a loving Father, "Every good thing bestowed and every perfect gift is from above" (James 1:17).

Through the ministry of James Jordan and his wife, I have learned to surrender any matter to a loving Father who cares for me. Now I watch in wonder as He works on my behalf. I am at peace, knowing God is going before me. He covers me under the shadow of His wings.

> I had been willing to eat the crumbs, but the Lord had real bread set aside for me…if I would only sit at the table with Him. "His banner over me is love…"
> *Song of Solomon 2:4a*

Our dads are supposed to go before us, protect and defend us. Earthly fathers are not perfect, and many fall short. The important thing is that God isn't like our earthly father…He is our Dad…Abba… Daddy. This is the very term Jesus used when speaking of God.

I remember sitting in my new kitchen making pizza shortly after arriving at the new place. The fragrant aroma went throughout the house, and at the end of the day, there wasn't one roach within a mile of it. Why? Because our Daddy cares.

For you have not received a spirit of slavery leading to fear again, but you have received a spirit of adoption as sons by which we cry out, "**Abba**! Father!"

—Rom. 8:15

Chapter 19

The Touch That Heals

The sun of righteousness will rise with healing in its wings; and you will go forth and skip about like calves from the stall.

—Mal. 4:2

Bless the LORD, O my soul, and all that is within me, bless His holy name. Bless the LORD, O my soul, and forget none of His benefits; who pardons all your iniquities, **who heals all your diseases**; who redeems your life from the pit, who crowns you with lovingkindness and compassion; who satisfies your years with good things, so that your youth is renewed like the eagle.

—Ps. 103:1-5

HE REMEMBERS YOU

HE HAD BEEN sitting at the gate of the temple for as long as he could remember. Carried in by family or friends each day, he sat...waiting, stretching out his hand, bearing a cup, asking for alms. This particular door where he sat, called the Beautiful Gate, went from the court of the Gentiles to the court of the women.[64] Day by day people

That is until one day... when something spectacular happened....

passed him. Some, moved with pity, quickly dropped a few coins in his wooden vessel and hurried off. Others pretended not to hear his petition as they passed.

With his head downcast, he saw vaguely the forms of two strong men pass him by. The time had arrived for the hour of prayer in the temple. Reaching out toward them, he asked for money, but God saw his need...his need for restoration. Peter, along with John, noticed him first and turned to face him. "Look at us!" Peter said. Slowly, the man raised his head, meeting the gaze of a strong fisherman. Fixing his gaze on him, Peter said, "I do not possess silver and gold, but what I do have I give to you: In the name of Jesus Christ the Nazarene—walk!" (Acts 3:6).

> And seizing him by the right hand, he raised him up; and immediately his feet and his ankles were strengthened. With a leap he stood upright and began to walk; and he entered the temple with them, walking and leaping and praising God. And all the people saw him walking and praising God; and they were taking note of him as being the one who used to sit at the Beautiful Gate of the temple to beg alms, and they were filled with wonder and amazement.
>
> —Acts 3:7-10

The man followed Peter and John, still amazed at being able to walk for the first time in his life. The people followed them, and at the portico of Solomon, Peter gave his second sermon. Even though the Sadducees had them arrested later, "many of those who had heard the message believed; and the number of men came to about five thousand" (Acts 4:4).

He was not passed by...

In the midst of all this glorious work God was doing, the man at the gate was healed. After years of waiting for a miracle or simply sustenance, God gave immeasurably beyond all he could ask or think.

IN THE NAME OF JESUS

Peter went on, "It is the name of Jesus which has strengthened this man whom you see and know; and the faith which comes through Him has given him this perfect health in the presence of you all" (Acts 3:16). According to the *IVP New Testament Commentary*:

> This serves only to heighten the value of the great gift he does offer: complete health. But it is *in the name of Jesus Christ of Nazareth* that it must be given. A name is an expression of a person's very essence. The power of the person is present and available in the name (Haenchen 1971:200). In the case of Jesus, the invocation of his name is a direct link between earth and heaven. It is not a magic formula but a simple recognition that if any salvation blessings are to come, they must arrive in and through the person of Jesus Christ.[65]

Matthew Henry's Concise Commentary echoes this thought:

> How sweet the thought to our souls, that in respect to all the crippled faculties of our fallen nature, the name of Jesus Christ of Nazareth can make us whole! With what holy joy and rapture shall we tread the holy courts, when God the Spirit causes us to enter therein by his strength!
>
> —Acts 3:12-18[66]

Heaven and earth meet in the name of Jesus! Many times, I recall asking God how a certain dilemma would be resolved. On a special occasion, my eyes instantly glanced at a horizontal line meeting a vertical one, and I saw the cross. In the name of Jesus we are healed and made whole.

> Just as a father has compassion on his children,
> So the LORD has compassion on those who fear Him. For He Himself knows our frame.
>
> —Ps. 103:13-14

REACHING FOR HOPE

For twelve years she had been in pain. She had tried everything, but no remedy had ever worked. While she was hemorrhaging, protocol dictated that she not appear in public. But He was here, they said. The healer, the prophet, the man called Jesus.

As she slowly arose and put on her outer garments, hope arose in her heart. She was desperate and said to herself, "If I only touch His garment, I will get well" (Matt. 9:21). She surveyed the street. If only she could reach Him. He was nearby, on His way to help a little girl.

Pushing through the crowd, she saw Him. She saw Him! Just a little bit closer. And then something happened. He saw her. In the midst of the pain and the misery, He gazed upon her and saw her crying out for help. She was desperate, and she was willing to risk a rebuke from the crowd. Her eyes met His and she felt herself go warm all over. "Jesus turning and seeing her said, 'Daughter, take courage; your faith has made you well.' At once the woman was made well" (Matt. 9:22). All those years of pain washed away in a single sentence! She sat gazing in wonder, basking in the love that overflowed and overwhelmed her...His peace. He had healed her!

In a similar account in the Book of Luke, we read: "Who is the one who touched Me?" (Luke 8:45). Jesus' eyes were searching through the crowd. The woman saw His radiant face, beautifully framed with a soft beard, and kind eyes. But before she could reply, Peter stepped in, "'Master, the people are crowding and pressing in on You.' But Jesus said, 'Someone did touch Me, for I was aware that power had gone out of Me'" (Luke 8:45-46).

> When the woman saw that **she had not escaped notice**, she came trembling and fell down before Him, and declared in the presence of all the people the reason why she had touched Him, and how she had been immediately healed.
>
> —Luke 8:47

According to *The New John Gill Exposition of the Entire Bible*:

> The Syriac and Arabic versions render it, "that he had not forgot her"; she hoping he would be diverted from taking any notice of her and her action, through the crowd of people about him;[67]

According to the Torah, this woman would have had to "take for herself two turtledoves or two young pigeons and bring them in to the priest, to the doorway of the tent of meeting" for a sin and a burnt offering eight days after her discharge had ceased (Lev. 15:29). All of this was done "so that they will not die in their uncleanness by their defiling My tabernacle that is among them" (Lev. 15:31).

She had not escaped His notice. When she touched Jesus, she was made clean.

God had seen her in the midst of the crowd and healed her. Jesus tenderly gazed at this one and spoke. "Daughter, your faith has made you well; go in peace" (Luke 8:48).

> The LORD is compassionate and gracious,
> Slow to anger and abounding in lovingkindness.
>
> —Ps. 103:8

STEADFAST FAITH

> For as high as the heavens are above the earth, so great is His lovingkindness toward those who fear Him.
>
> —Ps. 103:11

As he entered Capernaum, a centurion approached Jesus. He was a humble man, who had served Caesar, the Roman Emperor, faithfully in his occupation. Troubled, he approached Jesus. "Lord, my servant is lying paralyzed at home, fearfully tormented," he said (Matt. 8:6).

Jesus' response to the man was swift and concise. He simply said, "I will come and heal him." Yet before Jesus could do this, the centurion stopped him with these words of faith.

> Lord I am not worthy for You to come under my roof, but just say the word, and my servant will healed. For I also am a man under authority, with soldiers under me; and I say to this one, "Go!" and he goes, and to another, "Come!" and he comes, and to my slave, "Do this!" and he does it.
>
> —Matt. 8:8-9

The centurion had approximately one hundred military soldiers under him with some serving as domestics.[68] This servant was of concern to him. "Now when Jesus heard this, He marveled...Truly I say to you, I have not found such great faith with anyone in Israel'" (Matt. 8:10).

> Since (the centurion's) orders were immediately obeyed: how much more easily then could Christ, who had all power in heaven and in earth, command off this distemper his servant was afflicted with? Christ was subject to none. He (the centurion) suggests, that as his soldiers were under him, and at his command; so all bodily diseases were under Christ, and to be controlled by him, at his pleasure; and that, if he would but say to that servant of his, the palsy, remove, it would remove at once. [69]

"And Jesus said to the centurion, 'Go; it shall be done for you as you have believed.' And the servant was healed that very moment" (Matt. 8:13).

"All things are possible to him who believes."
Mark 9:23

GIVING THANKS

On His way to Jerusalem, Jesus came across ten lepers crying out for mercy. Moved with compassion, Jesus simply said, "Go and show yourselves to the priests" (Luke 17:14). As they did, something miraculous happened.

> As they were going, they were cleansed. Now one of them, when he saw that he had been healed, turned back, glorifying God with a loud voice, and he fell on his face at His feet, giving thanks to Him. And he was a Samaritan. Then Jesus answered and said, "Were there not ten cleansed? But the nine—where are they? Was no one found who returned to give glory to God, except this foreigner?"
> —Luke 17:14-18

The leper's first response had been thanksgiving. His leprosy had disappeared! He was eternally grateful to the one who had healed him.

As you go, preach, saying, "The kingdom of heaven at hand." Heal the sick, raise the dead, **cleanse the lepers**, cast out demons. Freely you have received, freely give.

—Matt. 10:7-8

A THANKFUL HEART

After wrapping up a great day of teaching, I was happy to go home. As I was packing up to leave, a student approached me apologizing for missing the last few classes. She had been diagnosed with kidney stones and had been in incredible pain. Norma was a gracious lady in her mid-fifties, and I could see from gazing in her eyes that she knew the Lord. "Would you like to pray?" I offered. Her eyes smiled back a grateful "yes."

As we were walking to my office, Shenita, another student, approached us in great distress. Her grandfather, the only father figure in her life, was in a coma. She, too, was in need of a Father's comfort. We huddled together for prayer in a tiny back room, falling into the arms of Jesus.

Norma was the first humbly to approach the Lord, petitioning Him on our behalf. We began to feel the strong and weighty presence of the Lord. We all rested in His presence and the Holy Spirit moved. After we each took turns praying, it was time to leave. Yet, we all knew we had been touched by God in a special way.

BREAKTHROUGH

Two days later, Shenita burst into one of my earlier classes. "My grandfather is awake! I went to visit him after we prayed, and he came out of his coma!" Tears still glisten in my eyes as I write this now some years later. She continued, "I had to come and tell you because I know God answered our prayer."

I began to cry. The Lord had given this young woman the guiding hand of a father figure in her life. In this age of promiscuity, where many girls raised without fathers look for love in the arms of a boy, Shenita would have the love of her grandfather. She would know that she was precious.

We hugged, thanking God for bringing him back into her life. Then she was off, smiling, to her next class. I could hear her humming all the way down the hall as she left. Curious, the next day I asked my other student about her visit with the doctor. She beamed, "The kidney stones are gone. If they passed, I never even felt them." She went on, "They must have dissolved, because the doctor cannot find them. It is a *miracle!*" "Incredible!" I replied, stunned. This was indeed a miracle since most people find passing a kidney stone to be more painful than childbirth. God, our loving Father, had heard and answered. He had truly met us by answering our prayers, and in the process, renewing my strength.

> Nor has He hidden His face from him; but when he cried to Him for help, He heard.
>
> —Ps. 22:24

IT'S NOT YOUR TIME YET

> I have seen his ways, but I will heal him; I will lead him and restore comfort to his mourners, creating the praise of the lips...and I will heal him.
>
> —Isa. 57:18-19

She was a young mother in her early thirties. The doctor checked her vital signs, and graciously spoke with the young woman's husband in the hallway. "This doesn't look good," the doctor explained to her husband of fourteen years. She had survived the rigors of the operation, but now they were having trouble stabilizing her. Then, unexpectedly, her vital readings flat-lined. With her parents at her side, she went home to be with the Lord.

There was no more pain for her. She smiled as she looked up and floated toward the light. Overwhelming love encompassed her. Meanwhile, her parents gently laid hands upon her and simply prayed the Lord's prayer. "Our Father, who art in heaven hallowed be Thy name..." Her father was a humble man of great faith who made a silent appeal to the Lord to restore his daughter. Her mother was also meekly pleading.

Without warning, this young mother felt herself returning to her pain-stricken form. Two grateful pair of eyes looked upon her with love, and then at each other before thanking the Lord. She was back! Thankfully, the Lord had seen from heaven and said, "It's not your time yet," much to the joy of her daughter...me.

FAITHFUL FRIEND

Now fast-forward fifteen years. The diagnosis: a tumor the size of a grapefruit rested inside her. We began to pray, asking God for a miracle. My mother, meanwhile, was at such peace with God that my father scratched his head in wonder. It truly was "the peace of God, which surpasses all comprehension" (Phil. 4:7).

On the day of her surgery, I received a call. Puzzled, since it was only four hours since her surgery began, I asked Mom how she was feeling. "Great!" she replied, somewhat on Vicodin. She continued. "The tumor is gone! Three days before the surgery, I believed God could heal me, and He did! I felt this bursting sensation and I knew God had healed me! The doctors still needed to treat another area for something else, but not the tumor. Woohoo! I am so happy!"

Tears of gratitude gently rolled down my cheeks as I heard the news. God is Jehovah Rapha, our healer.

For You heard my cry, and You answered me.
—IHOP Limited Edition

Facing the Giants

He [David]… chose for himself five smooth stones from the brook,
and put them in the shepherd's bag which he had, even in his pouch,
and his sling was in his hand; and he approached the Philistine.
—1 Sam. 17:40

PEACE, NOT PANIC

CELIA DID NOT come to our first class of the semester; she came
to the second. Tentatively, this petite, young lady approached me at
the end of class. "Prrrrrofffessor JJJJJJooyyy," she stammered. "My my
my nananame is Cececelia." Gazing at this delightful student with the
pleading, brown eyes, I was touched. It had taken great courage for
her to enroll in this class. Stuttering, she explained that her advisor
had insisted she enroll in public speaking. She was required to finish it
successfully before she could graduate, and she was only one semester
away from celebrating that date.

Not only did she take panic attack medication, but she was terrified
of public speaking. For the first time in my teaching career, I was very
concerned. *Will she make it through the class?* I wondered. *I have never
heard anyone stutter this badly.* It had taken her five minutes to explain a
few simple ideas to me. I looked at anther student standing nearby, and

he nodded, offering some words of encouragement. When they left, I prayed. "God, I need Your help to help her. Show me, Lord, what I can do. It will take a miracle to get her through this."

The first speech was an icebreaker where you introduce another student. Since she had missed the first class, she would unfortunately have to introduce herself. Stepping slowly up to the podium, I watched her shake. *Dear Lord, please let her not have a panic attack,* I silently appealed.

Nervously, she glanced up at the class. After saying her name, she was ready to sit down again. Quickly, I smiled and walked to the podium to stand beside her. "It's all right. Celia is just a little nervous. After all, some studies say people are more afraid of speaking than death." The class laughed. "Now, why don't some of you ask Celia questions about herself?"

The class was incredibly supportive. When Celia forgot her note cards for her second speech, the class asked her questions to get her through it. By her third speech, she was dressing professionally and organizing her information well. The only real problem, the other students told her on their critiques, was that she "stuttered a little."

Stuttering is simply thinking of two things at once. Usually, the person is thinking about what they are going to say and wondering if they look ridiculous while they are doing it. It is rooted in the fear of man, rejection, and condemnation. If you couple that with panic attacks, you need a real breakthrough. Thus, providing a safe environment where students feel loved and accepted is needed and biblical. Again, "perfect love casts out all fear" (1 John 4: 18).

A SEASON FOR MIRACLES

Finally, the day came when students had to watch themselves on videotape. Celia put her DVD in the player at home, watched it for thirty seconds, and then immediately called her husband laughing hysterically…"Honey, I looked like an idiot," she said through giggles. Her worst fears had been realized as she stuttered her way through the speech, yet the class had been nothing but encouraging.

When Celia stood to deliver her last speech, a miracle had happened. This beautiful, young woman stood before the class, smiling. Her eyes swept the audience tenderly as she spoke, and her posture was humbly confident.

She did not stutter once.

God had broken through the fear, anxiety, and shame. He had delivered Celia. Now, she stood before me, a victorious woman. Grateful, she thanked her husband, the class for their inordinate support, and me. Meanwhile, through tears, I thanked God for what He had done.

Not all of my students' stories are so dramatic, but Celia's was.

LET JESUS LEAD

So that He might sanctify her, having cleansed her by the washing of water with the word.

—Eph. 5:26

Coming to Christ, as Neil Andersen states in *The Common Made Holy*, is like getting a new computer. The hardware totally changes. The software, however, is what needs to be continually rewritten.[70] According to Ephesians 5:26, "the washing of water with the Word" is what purifies us. We have to stop inserting that old floppy disk or zip drive or downloading the same old applications. We need to feed our minds with new material so that we become more like Christ. That is how the system runs on all cylinders. Did you know that your brain actually rewires itself whenever you change a pattern or behavior? It gradually changes physically to match your input spiritually.

It is important to remove the legal ground where the enemy may have a foothold by examining generational curses, ungodly beliefs, and soul/spirit hurts. *Restoring the Foundations* is an excellent counseling series to use in your local church as it encourages folks to take a very thorough approach to the start of healing.[71] When the legal ground is eliminated, the devil has no choice but to leave. Verbally speaking and renouncing any place you have come into agreement with the lies of the enemy is an important part of this process. God spoke the universe into existence, and in the early church, new converts renounced past ties to the enemy.

I love what Mike Bickle has to say on the subject of spiritual strongholds.

> Paul uses the term to describe any thinking that exalts itself above the knowledge of God, giving the enemy a protected place of influence in a person's thought life...A stronghold in the mind is a collection of thoughts in agreement with Satan-thought that are lies against what God has revealed about Himself. [72]

So, in essence, it is an area of your thought life that needs the light of God's presence. I picture a house in which the lights are on in some rooms, but not in others. The dark rooms just need an invasion of light. One flick of the light switch, one Word of God's truth can pierce the darkness. The darkness has to flee.

God identifies areas in our lives that still need healing or total sanctification. By feeding on His truth, we begin to see ourselves as He sees us: a new creation. Corey Russell of the International House of Prayer recently commented at their annual One Thing Conference that it is not enough to cast out demons; we must replace the lies we believed with truth by feeding ourselves on the Word of God.[73] Remember, it is the "washing of water with the Word." We must eat the scroll so to speak.

> "You will know the truth, and the truth will make you free."
> *John 8:32*

God has forgiven us of our sin, so sin no longer has dominion over us. "Nay, in all these things we are more than conquerors through him who loved us" (Rom. 8:37 KJV). We no longer live the same way. Through Christ we have the ability to say "no" to sin. "Greater is He who is in you than he who is in the world" (1 John 4:4).

What does this mean? "Submit therefore to God resist the devil and he will flee from you" (James 4:7). For most of my adult life, I spent time focusing on kicking the enemy out if there was a sin or temptation, rather than first appealing to God for help. The first step is submission.

Open your spirit to God first, seeking His aid first. Wait on Him. Pour your heart out to Him. Usually, by that time, the oppression or negative thought has fled. But the first step is always surrendering the matter to God.

Imagine a boat with a rudder, and once you surrender your life, your will, and your love to the Lord, He takes over manning that rudder. Your life can take a completely different direction from what you first thought. Yet, giving Him the helm is the wisest decision of your life. Let Jesus lead. Now as the waves come or the waters grow rough, you are in the boat with Him as He steers. He is your peace.

> I have been crucified with Christ; and it is no longer I who live, but Christ lives in me; and the life which I now live in the flesh I live by faith in the Son of God, who **loved** me and gave **Him**self up for me.
> —Gal. 2:20

AN ADVOCATE

> Or what man is there among you who, when his son asks for a loaf, will give him a stone? If you then, being evil, know how to give good gifts to your children, how much more will your Father who is in heaven give what is good to those who ask Him!
> —Matt. 7:9, 11

She was desperate. Leaving her house in the district of Tyre and Sidon, she went in pursuit of the one they called Jesus. Searching the streets, she asked local merchants and townspeople if they had seen Him. Indeed many had, and several directed her toward the crowds following after Jesus. Renewed in strength, she pressed on to find Him. She knew He could heal her daughter. Lifting her dress slightly, she continued to run, oblivious to all else.

He was speaking to His disciples about a matter regarding the Pharisees. Heedlessly, she began to push through the crowd. "'Have mercy on me, Lord, Son of David; my daughter is cruelly demon-possessed.'

And then she saw Him.

But He did not answer her a word" (Matt. 15:22-23). Still, she continued shouting. It did not matter that she got little response or that the others frowned at her. He was the answer! And she knew it.

Finally, the other disciples began to encourage Jesus to ask her to leave, for her cries for mercy were unrelenting. Turning to gaze upon her, Jesus answered her, "I was sent only to the lost sheep of the house of Israel" (Matt. 15:24).

Not put off, for she was a Canaanite woman, she replied, "Lord, help me" (Matt. 15:25). Again Jesus took His time responding, "It is not good to take the children's bread and throw it to the dogs" (Matt. 15:26). Hearing such a remark, most would have grown offended at the delay. Scholars suggest that Jesus was testing her, to see if she would relent or believe. Yet this woman was unmoved. From where she knelt, she lifted her eyes and said firmly,

> "Yes, Lord; but even the dogs feed on the crumbs which fall from their masters' table." Then Jesus said to her, "O woman, your faith is great; it shall be done for you as you wish." **And her daughter was healed at once**.
>
> —Matt. 15:27-28

Her daughter was healed! This Canaanite woman wanted something so desperately that she was willing to bear any humiliation to receive the answer to her prayers. She was pleading for the life of her child. Nothing could get in her way. Her focus was on Jesus, the One before her. So she cried out to Him, awaiting His answer.

While writing this, I happened to click onto the International House of Prayer service. There I beheld a young woman draped in a beautiful, bluish shawl about her head and shoulders, worshipping before the Lord. It was the perfect picture of the image of holy abandonment before a merciful and compassionate God.

LIFE LESSONS

Students had been presenting speeches that commemorated a relative, friend, or legend who had impacted their lives. The stories they shared were powerful ones, but having taught this class many times in the past, I was struggling with keeping it fresh. Then one day, several things happened that marked the beginning of many special days with those students.

The previous week, I had been stressed out, focused on the little things that went wrong. As I walked into that classroom, I was reminded that each one of these precious students was made in God's image. They were to be honored and cared for as such. I needed to lay aside my concern for getting the cameras that I used to record them set up properly and on time, and instead, remember why I was doing this in the first place. My eyes had been opened again to the power of God's love. As the students made themselves vulnerable, hearts were touched in a special way.

One young man spoke of his wonderful mother and how she had shared Christ with him. He was so full of joy that we all assumed she was alive. His demeanor did not change as he disclosed her life's story to us. It was a part of his testimony that he was not bitter, but truly joyful even in disclosing her death two years prior. I watched the class's reaction, expecting sadness at the loss of his mother or even anger with God over the matter. Since this was not evident, they marveled, wondering where such strength could come from. Kevin knew with confidence where his mother was and that he would see her again in heaven. These students were seeing the power of a changed life when we surrender to Christ.

Amy also had the spotlight that day. She had brought her mentor (the wife of a pastor) to class so that she could personally present her with an award. It was a touching moment not lost on the class. Through their transparency, I could see God breaking into and going through their hearts. Hearts were opening; the fields were white for harvest.

Ashley was last to go that day. A sweet, smiling young lady, she always sat at the front of the class with her best friend and roommate, Brittany. When it was her turn to speak, Ashley hesitantly rose and took her place behind the podium. As the camera crew got ready to record her speech, Ashley's pent-up anxiety was finally released. A slow, but steady stream of tears began to flow down her cheeks. Since many of the speeches had been deeply moving, most of the class mistook Ashley's tears for tears of sadness, not alarm.

"This is her worst fear," Brittany whispered to me. I understood.

"Lord," I silently prayed. "Help me. Help her. Show me what to do. I am at a loss, Lord."

In the meantime, with tears still streaming down her cheeks, Ashley looked pleadingly at me, "I can't," she said simply.

"Brittany," I whispered back, "go and stand beside her while she speaks." Dutifully, Brittany did. This seemed to ease Ashley's fears somewhat; the two had done all of their speeches together.

"Yes, you can, Ashley. You talk all the time," Brittany said, nudging her friend. After what seemed to be minutes, Ashley began to speak. It was as if someone had uncorked a bottle. Once opened, everything just naturally flowed out. It was truly something to see.

The next class, Ashley beamed up at me as I walked past the front row. Her eyes radiated joy. "I am so proud of you," I said, handing her back the graded critique sheet. She smiled a brilliant smile in return. This had been a victory for her too.

Chapter 21

Total Forgiveness

But You are a God of **forgiveness**, gracious and compassionate, slow to anger and abounding in lovingkindness; and You did not forsake them.

—Neh. 9:17

BAND OF BROTHERS

WITH HOPE IN their hearts, a band of friends carried in a paralyzed man on a bed. They had heard of this man, Jesus. He healed the sick, raised the dead, and cast out demons. Surely, He could heal their friend. "Seeing their faith, Jesus said to the paralytic, 'Take courage, son; your sins are forgiven'" (Matt. 9:2). Upon hearing this, the scribes were outraged, believing that Jesus had blasphemed against God.

> And Jesus knowing their thoughts said, "Why are you thinking evil in your hearts? Which is easier, to say, 'Your sins are forgiven,' or to say, 'Get up, and walk?' But so that you may know that the Son of Man has authority on earth to forgive sins"—then He said to the paralytic, "Get up, pick up you bed and go home." And he got up and went home. But when the crowds saw this, they were awestruck, and glorified God, who had given such authority to men.
>
> —Matt. 9:4-8

Jesus healed the paralytic man, but he was more concerned with something else—the man's sins. We see this theme of sin being dealt with repeatedly in Scripture as in the story of the healing of the man at the pool of Bethesda.

GET UP AND WALK!

Another man had been waiting by the pool of Bethesda some thirty-eight years in the hopes of being healed. Jesus saw him and His words to him were few. "Do you wish to get well?" The man had replied that this was his heart's desire, and so Jesus' simple response was, "Get up, pick up your pallet and walk" (John 5:6, 8). After the Jews questioned the now-healed man, Jesus found him later in the temple. He said to the man, "Behold, you have become well; do not sin anymore, so that nothing worse happens to you" (John 5:14).

WHY FORGIVENESS?

Research has shown that the sin of unforgiveness is often at the root of a physical ailment.[74] Remember we are body, soul, and spirit; the three intertwine. Communion is offered at the International House of Prayer before any physical needs are ministered to in the healing rooms. We must examine ourselves and remove any hindrance that keeps us from God's love. Jesus said in that telling prayer, "Forgive us our sins, for we ourselves also forgive everyone who is indebted to us" (Luke 11:4). We must forgive so that we can be forgiven.

Perhaps the best book I have ever read on this subject of forgiveness is R.T. Kendall's *Total Forgiveness*.[75] I cannot recommend it highly enough. It is important that we forgive others, God, and in some cases, ourselves. To harbor unforgiveness is like drinking the poison you intended for your enemy. The physical ramifications are tremendous. Not only this, but unforgiveness affects our intimacy with God.

A POWERFUL WITNESS

Jesus was persecuted, and yet He was innocent. Some of His last words on the cross were, "Father, forgive them; for they do not know what they are doing" (Luke 23:34). Remember the story of the two debtors in Matthew 18:21-35? The parallel is that since He has forgiven us so great a debt, how can we help but forgive others for what they have done to us?

It is true that Jesus healed others for the glory of God, as in the case of the man born blind. He said, "It was neither that this man sinned, nor his parents; but it was so that the works of God might be displayed in him" (John 9:3). Thus, the remainder of that passage deals with how this man gave testimony to God's faithfulness in the courts of the Jews. Should we have any sin in our heart, we definitely need to leave it at the cross.

FREE TO FORGIVE

> Blessed are you when people insult you and persecute you, and falsely say all kinds of evil against you because of Me. Rejoice and be glad, for your reward in heaven is great; for in the same way they persecuted the prophets who were before you.
>
> —Matt. 5:11

He was a young man greatly favored by his father, and he was his mother's first child. They took great delight in him, bouncing him upon their knees and smiling shyly at each other. They were in love, and this was their first son. As the boy grew, his father lavished his love upon him. Smiling tenderly at his wife, Jacob sighed. This was their beloved son. His beautiful wife radiated a profound sense of joy. She and the man she loved finally had the child for which they had longed. As the years went by, they would have another, but Joseph would always have a special place in his father's heart.

Rachel had been Jacob's first choice, but she was his second wife. Although he had worked seven years to earn Rachel's hand in marriage, on the eve of his wedding, Laban sent his elder daughter, Leah, to Jacob. After the wedding night, when Jacob awoke, he beheld Leah and not Rachel. Imagine his pain! Jacob served another seven years in order to wed Rachel. Although he was officially married to both women, Jacob still had eyes only for Rachel.

Leah longed for her husband's love. Despite Laban's treachery, God heard Leah's cry and had mercy on her.

> Now the Lord saw that Leah was unloved, and He opened her womb, but Rachel was barren. Leah conceived and bore a son and named him Reuben, for she said, "Because the Lord has seen my affliction; surely now my husband will love me."
>
> —Gen. 29: 31-32

Leah went on to bear Jacob six sons and a daughter, always with the idea that after the birth of each, her husband would come to love her. But this was not to be. Jacob had loved Rachel from the beginning.

Envision what it must have been like as one of Leah's children. Imagine watching your mother grieve, year after year, that she was not beloved of Jacob. Watching Leah's heartbreak over and over again must have angered her sons. Later, Joseph paid a great penalty for their sins.

As a young boy, God gave Joseph dreams. In each of his dreams, his brothers and family bowed to him. This angered Joseph's brothers. They were already jealous of the treatment he received from their father, and they were grieved by the way Jacob overlooked their mother, Leah, in favor of Rachel.

This deep animosity bore fruit later as Joseph's brothers ambushed him. Throwing him into a pit, they stripped him of the precious coat his beloved father had just given him. Rather than kill him, Judah finally voted to sell him into slavery to some Midianite traders passing by. The others agreed, and when Reuben, the eldest again arrived on the scene to rescue his brother, Joseph was already gone.

Fast-forward years later. God has given Joseph favor after years of testing—first, in Potiphar's house where he managed the estate until Potiphar's wife falsely accuses him of adultery. Then he is thrust in prison on false charges, where he continues to serve faithfully.

> But the Lord was with Joseph and extended kindness to him, and gave him favor in the sight of the chief jailer. The chief jailer committed to Joseph's charge all the prisoners who were in jail; so that whatever was done there, he was responsible for it. The chief jailer did not supervise

anything under Joseph's charge because the Lord was with him; and whatever he did, the Lord made to prosper.

—Gen. 39:21-23

While serving there, Joseph meets two of the king's servants, the chief cupbearer and the baker. After interpreting dreams for both men, the chief cupbearer is released. Years later, when Pharaoh has a dream, the cupbearer remembers Joseph. He is called forth to interpret the dream's meaning.

Joseph interprets Pharaoh's dream, stating that God is warning them of an approaching famine. They must prepare and set aside grain for the seasons when there will not be plenty. Pharaoh heeds Joseph's words and elevates Joseph to a position of high authority. "Since God has informed you of all this, there is no one so discerning and wise as you are. You shall be over my house…See, I have set you over all the land of Egypt" (Gen. 41:39-41).

Now enter Joseph's brothers. The famine has struck their homeland. Jacob's family journeys to Egypt to buy food, for "Joseph stored up grain in great abundance like the sand of the sea, until he stopped measuring it, for it was beyond measure" (Gen. 41:49). When they arrive, Joseph recognizes them, but does not reveal his identity until later when they return, bringing his little brother, Benjamin, with them. "Then Joseph could not control himself before all those who stood by him" (Gen. 45:1). So Joseph sent everyone out except his brothers so that he could reveal himself to them. Scripture says that, "he wept so loudly that the Egyptians heard it, and the household of Pharaoh heard of it" (Gen. 45:2). Then Joseph spoke to his brothers.

> "Forgive us our sins, for we ourselves also forgive everyone who is indebted to us."
> *Luke 11:4*

I am your brother Joseph, whom you sold into Egypt. Now do not be grieved or angry with yourselves, because you sold me here, **for God sent me before you to preserve life.** For the famine has been in the land these two years, and there are still five years in which there will be neither plowing nor harvesting. **God sent me before you to preserve for you a remnant in the earth, and to keep you alive by a great deliverance.**

—Gen. 45:4-7

All those years, all that pain, and yet, Joseph had forgiven his brothers. He held nothing against them. God was painting a greater picture. "Now, therefore, it was not you who sent me here, but God" (Gen. 45:8). Joseph's character had been tested and formed in Egypt, in Potiphar's house and in prison. He was free to love and help them now after forgiving them.

Chapter 22

My Daily Bread

NOTHING IS TOO hard for the Lord to do. As Paul declared that God is able "to do far more abundantly beyond all that we ask or think" (Eph. 3:20).

E.M. Bounds reflecting on Ephesians 3:20

There will always be enough.
Word of the Lord to Heidi Baker

IT NEVER RUNS OUT!

> Now a certain woman of the wives of the sons of the prophets cried out to Elisha, "Your servant my husband is dead, and you know that your servant feared the LORD; and the creditor has come to take my two children to be his slaves.
>
> —2 Kings 4:1

She was a woman in desperate circumstances. Her husband, a good man, had passed away, leaving her in a difficult situation with a debt to repay. Alas, the creditor had sworn to take away her two precious children in repayment of the debt! This thought, which seems extraordinary, was prevalent in the ancient world and still occurs in some places even today.

Despite the loss of her husband, she drew her strength from a deep love and trust in God. She and her husband had been faithful to serve the Lord, for her husband was the son of a prophet. She had seen many things in her lifetime, and all of them pointed to the fact that God was her rock and that He would provide for her and her family. Thus, this woman of faith went in search of one who could help her.

Being an honorable woman, she went in pursuit of the man of God. As she approached, Elisha noted her countenance. She was solemn, explaining what had happened. She completely trusted that God would rescue her in this moment of need. Elisha gazed at her steadfastness.

> "What shall I do for you? Tell me, what do you have in the house?" And she said, "Your maidservant has nothing in the house except a jar of oil." Then he said, "Go, borrow vessels at large for yourself from all your neighbors, even empty vessels; do not get a few. And you shall go in and shut the door behind you and your sons, and pour out into all these vessels, and you shall set aside what is full."
>
> —2 Kings 4:2-4

And so, she and her children did just that. After gathering vessels from neighbors and friends, she sequestered herself and her children in a room, and began to pour. Miraculously as she, in faith, lifted the jar of oil and tipped it downward, oil flowed out until all the vessels in her house were filled! All she had left in her household was a small, simple jar of oil, having sold all her other valuable items. God multiplied its use.

When she returned to the man of God, joy filled her heart. Elisha said, "Go, sell the oil and pay your debt, and you and your sons can live on the rest" (2 Kings 4:7). God had provided miraculously on her behalf!

> He had seen her need and what was available to her and multiplied it.

SPRINGTIME AND HARVEST

According to UNICEF, there is enough food in the world for everyone to have a 2,500-calorie diet each day. According to theologian David

Pawson, the problem is that we won't share. In the early church, each gave freely, helping those in need. No social programs would be needed today if we as a church would follow Christ's example.[76]

> And the congregation of those who believed were of one heart and soul; and not one of them claimed that anything belonging to him was his own, but all things were common property to them. And with great power the apostles were giving testimony to the resurrection of the Lord Jesus, and abundant grace was upon them all. For there was not a needy person among them, for all who were owners of land or houses would sell them and bring the proceeds of the sales and lay them at the apostles' feet, and they would be distributed to each as any had need.
>
> —Acts 4:32-35

In the Book of Acts, the new church gave freely, helping those in need. Here, according to Pawson, we are released from the tithe, which falls under the Mosaic covenant. Previously, the Jewish people were asked to give ten percent of their income or first fruits. In Acts, we see a shift, where believers can give as much as they want. "God loves a cheerful giver." He is not interested in your pocketbook, but your heart. Remember the widow who gave all (as little as it was in comparison with the Pharisees' gifts)? "For they all put in out of their surplus, but she, out of her poverty, put in all she owned" (Mark 12:44).

So one-third of the world goes to bed hungry, another one-third goes to bed starving, and the last one-third goes to bed full. Under the Noahic covenant, God promised we would always have, "springtime and harvest." God has been faithful to keep His side of the bargain. He provides, and we should give out of our abundance. "Give one child all the candy to distribute to the others, and he won't share more than a little," says Pawson.[77] The truth is that we need our hearts to be pierced as Agabus's was in the New Testament.

> One of them named Agabus stood up and began to indicate by the Spirit that there would certainly be a great famine all over the world. And this took place in the reign of Claudius. **And in proportion that**

any of disciples had means, each of them determined to send a contribution for the relief of the brethren in Judea.

—Acts 11:28-29

RELENTLESS

There was a widow in that city, and she kept coming to him and saying, "Give me legal protection from my opponent." For a while he was unwilling; but afterward he said to himself, "Even though I do not fear God nor respect man, yet because this widow bothers me, I will give her legal protection, otherwise by continually coming she will wear me out."

—Luke 18:3-5

During a revival meeting on campus, the Lord showed me a vision of heaven. I saw Jesus standing beside a small child, holding his hand. A graduate class was preparing to shoot a brief pro-life film, and I had asked for a vision of what the Lord wished to do. "Tell his story," the Lord solemnly charged. "Whose story, Lord?" I asked. "The mother's, the father's... "No," the Lord gently prodded. "Tell his story." And He referenced the little boy.

Tears began to stream down my face. I left that meeting and began to sketch out a brief piece that was a radical departure from an earlier story line. Its message was of a grace, beauty, and forgiveness that I had never seen before.

The vision before me was the story, told from a child's perspective, of a couple's love for each other and their discovery of a new life growing within. A young child narrates how his parents met, fell in love, and grew to care for each other. Throughout, the child has been speaking of his love for his parents, especially his mother. We see the couple becoming more intimate and then—there is a jarring conversation. The young woman, upon discovering that she is pregnant, deliberates with her fiancé what she should do. We see her sense of hopelessness and shame as she, through tears, turns away from him while he tries to comfort her. Still, since the child has been speaking to us throughout everything, it is safe to assume he will be all right.

Then we cut to an abortion clinic. The mother is being led down a long hall. We see her hesitancy. She turns back briefly as her lover rises from his chair with hope in his heart that she's changed her mind. She gives him one last look. We wait to see what will unfold. Shaking her head mournfully and steeling herself against defeat, she enters the room. We see her positioned in the stirrups as preparations are made. And then…a scream. Cut to black.

As the lights come back up, we see her now, weeping on the floor in her home as her fiancé, also in shock, tries to comfort her. Fade to white. From the moment she enters the clinic, we ceased hearing the little boy's voice. As we fade away from the couple, a blinding light fills the screen.

Now, we see a little boy robed in white walking toward someone. He has brown hair, beautiful blue eyes, and a gentle demeanor. "I miss my mommy," he says walking along gently. Then he looks up to see someone waiting for him. "But I hope to see her one day in heaven." These are the final words of the child as he enters heaven and is received by Jesus. Jesus gently strokes his head as the child embraces Him.

The story was so powerful that I continued to behold its message as we pursued all the necessary things to make the vision possible. Our prayer as a film crew was to communicate this message of forgiveness and grace to young mothers for whom this tragedy was real.

We were blessed. In the midst of a hectic shooting schedule with other classes overlapping and needing similar crewmembers and equipment, the best cinematographers, grips, camera operators, and editors stepped forward to help. Every four hours new volunteers appeared to aid us. Only a few core members remained for the entire two days of shooting. Not only this, but the weather was perfectly fair for our outdoor shots. Miracle after miracle occurred, and we all felt the sweet presence of the Lord as we did this work for Him.

We needed a space that would double as an abortion clinic. After several phone calls, two options arose the day before we were supposed to shoot those graphic scenes. One location was willing, but insisted on drawing up legal papers in case we caused any damage to their property. While I was on the phone with them, another call came in. A local chiropractor, friends with the local Crisis Pregnancy Center, freely offered his entire office. As we filmed, he not only offered to get us Boston Market food should we wish it, but he took several crew members into a room and gave them a free massage on a self-propelled massage bed. Just one click of the switch and their worries melted away. It was more than we could have ever asked for.

Since we had only a little over two rolls of film on which to shoot everything, all the scenes had to be rehearsed until they were ready to be filmed. The actors followed the leading of the Holy Spirit, giving performances that communicated the heart of the piece.

I knew, as the film's producer, that we were in need of the school's grip truck to complete the shoot smoothly. It did not bother me that the truck was only loaned out for a spring or summer student film and this was fall. We needed it. Finally, the professor in charge of that class approved the use of the grip truck. His response as he handed me the keys was a memorable one. "You were like the persistent widow. And that is why I gave it to you."

> Whatever you ask in My name, that will I do, so that the Father may be glorified in the Son.
>
> —John 14:13

Chapter 23

Just Believe

Faith is the assurance of things hoped for, the conviction of things not seen.

—Heb. 11:1

ON THE MOVE

Let morning bring me word of your unfailing love, for I have put my trust in you. Show me the way I should go, for to you I lift up my soul.

—Ps. 143:8 NIV

IMAGINE BEING TOLD to go somewhere you have never been, yet knowing that God has something in store. Abraham lived in tents like a nomad most of his life...yet he was faithful to obey. "For he was looking for the city which has foundations, whose architect and builder is God" (Heb. 11:10).

> "For we walk by faith, not by sight."
> *2 Cor. 5:7*

This always reminds me of the scene in Indiana Jones where Jones is forced to take a leap of faith in stepping out onto an invisible bridge. The bridge is there waiting to catch him; it is just hidden from the naked eye by the rocks. Once Indiana is obedient to leap, the provision is there. In fact, it was there all the time; he just couldn't see it. I recall Jones's look of relief as he scatters more rocks across the bridge, so that he can see the rest of the pathway more clearly.

I think faith is like that. The more we read God's Word and learn who He is, the more secure we are in the knowledge that He loves us and keeps His word. Sometimes, like Job, we encounter a season of character testing, but truly these "momentary afflictions" are crafting a vessel that glorifies His heart. As we walk by faith, He is glorified and we expect and live differently than we would have before. Sometimes, as when the priests approached the water, it was not until they stepped into the Jordan that the waters receded.

SPYING OUT THE LAND

> Consecrate yourselves, for tomorrow the LORD will do wonders among you.
>
> —Josh. 3:5

Joshua means Yahweh is salvation.[78] He was one of the spies sent into the Promised Land who returned with a favorable report to give to Moses. He believed God had prepared the land for them. When the Israelites rebelled and fearfully believed the bad report given by some of the other spies, Joshua stood fast. With the passing of Moses, the mantle of leadership fell to Joshua to lead the nation of Israel into the Promised Land at last.

> "Come here, and hear the words of the LORD your God." Joshua said, "By this you shall know that the living God is among you, and that He will assuredly dispossess from before you the Canaanite, the Hittite, the Hivite, the Perizzite, the Girgashite, the Amorite, and the Jebusite."
>
> —Josh 3:9-10

Now, God gave them a sign ahead of time to show them that He loved them and to strengthen their faith. What blessed assurance!

Behold, the ark of the covenant of the Lord of all the earth is crossing over ahead of you into the Jordan. Now then, take for yourselves twelve men from the tribes of Israel, one man for each tribe. It shall come about when the soles of the feet of the priests who carry the ark of the Lord, the Lord of all the earth, rest in the waters of the Jordan, the waters of the Jordan will be cut off, and the waters which are flowing down from above will stand in one heap.

—Josh. 3:11-13

Many think of this miracle as one akin to the parting of the Red Sea while Moses and the Israelites crossed and escaped the Egyptians. But this miracle differed in its scope. When the priests, bearing the Ark of the Covenant, stepped into the water at the Jordan, the waters were cut off nineteen miles away from them! So for a stretch of that many miles, the Israelites were able to walk across a riverbed! Professor Chris Cunningham posed the question, "Now why would God do this except to show Himself mighty before the nations? So that everyone could see His glory."[79]

A SIGN AND A WONDER

Since ancient times no one has heard, no ear has perceived, no eye has seen any God besides you, who acts on behalf of those who wait for Him.

—Isa. 64:4 NIV

After crossing the Jordan, God commanded Joshua to have a member from each of the twelve tribes of Israel retrieve a stone from the place where the priests stood in the middle of the Jordan! Part of me wonders what it could have been like standing as a priest in the middle of a dry riverbed. Did any of them think, "Okay, everybody has crossed he river. Now we can get out of here! Not yet? Does anyone hear the sound of rushing water? No? I was just checking." It is funny to contemplate, but nothing is mentioned in Scripture to even hint at unbelief. They were fully confident. These men were totally surrendered to the mission and were secure as they held the Ark knowing that God had ordained this. In fact, God had said to Joshua, "This day I will begin to exalt you in the sight of all Israel, **that they may know that just as I have been with Moses, I will be with you**" (Josh. 3:7).

Thus, God commanded them to retrieve memorial stones. These stones would be carried to the place across the Jordan where the Israelites now lodged and placed in a heap. God's intention was clear; He was creating a memorial of His faithfulness.

> Let this be a sign among you, so that when your children ask later saying, "What do these stones mean to you?" then you shall say to them, "Because the waters of the Jordan were cut off before the ark of the covenant of the Lord; when it crossed the Jordan, the waters of the Jordan were cut off." So these stones shall become a memorial to the sons of Israel forever.
>
> —Josh. 4:6-7

These were memorial stones to help the Israelites in future generations remember what the Lord had done on their behalf. I think we too, like the Israelites who wandered in the wilderness, need to be reminded of God's great faithfulness in our lives. It is a way of stirring our remembrance. Something that will remind us—that will stir our memories and hearts the truth of God's provision, acceptance, and love.

We all need memorial stones.

As I took communion recently, Jesus' words, "Do this in remembrance of Me," struck me for the first time. Communion... total forgiveness...a reminder of the cross... His sacrifice...God's covenant with us. It is perfect that as part of the betrothal process in Jewish families, the bridegroom offered a cup of wine to the prospective bride. If she chose to accept it, the two drank from the same cup and became officially engaged. Accordingly:

> *The Betrothal (Kiddushin)* was derived from the word Kadosh, meaning holy. Once a bride and groom enter into this initial phase of marriage **they were considered married** and only legal divorce could break the betrothal. The betrothal was sealed with the 'cup of acceptance', which was a cup of wine offered to the bride by the groom. The groom left

to prepare the wedding room (Chuppah) and the Bride entered into a time of preparation and waiting including washings (Mikveh), the wearing of veil, undistracted devotion and great anticipation.[80]

> We need to build altars of remembrance.

Today, we have wedding rings to remind us of the sacred covenant of marriage. But as you take the cup for communion next time, I encourage you to remember Jesus offering it to you as a sign of the new covenant saying, "I am betrothed to you forever. I am marrying you, and I will never break my covenant. Will you marry me?"

Even When You Can't See It

For we walk by faith, not by sight.

—2 Cor. 5:7

Noah built an ark. Scientists estimate it was 450 feet long by 75 feet wide by 45 feet high. Now that's some ark! Thirty-six tennis courts could fit onto its deck alone! [81] The film *Evan Almighty* does a fairly good job of approximating the overall size of the ark. In fact, it was so immense in its final form that in the movie a famous theme park originally contracted to pick it up but then retracted the offer upon seeing its incredible size.[82]

> By faith Noah, being warned by God about things not yet seen, in reverence prepared an ark for the salvation of his household.
>
> —Heb. 11:7

Now there's a key…**by faith**. In the days preceding the flood, water rose in the morning (dew) and watered the earth.[83] There had never been any rain. For the people of Noah's day, the idea of rain falling from the sky was a new concept. Now couple that with God's assurance that there would be a flood! You can only imagine the persecution Noah must have endured.

Picture folks walking by Noah while he is taking a coffee break. "Hey Noah, what are you doing?" they asked him, laughing. Gazing at the huge ship before them, one might remark, "So, this is an ark. You're building an ark." One neighbor turned to another, puzzled. "Why are you building an ark?" Noah might patiently explain God's plan. Still puzzled, another friend might ask forcefully, "What do you mean it's going to rain and flood?" A pause. "By the way, what's rain?"

Yet, in love, God had instructed Noah to build the ark for the protection of himself and his family. Early shipbuilders actually modeled their vessels after the ark in their dimensions, etc. So, the long and the short of it is that God actually does know everything, and His promises are true. He does not lie. He speaks the truth. So if God has promised something to you, He will fulfill it—*in his time.*

PREPARE FOR RAIN

In a famous scene in the film, *Facing the Giants,* the protagonist, a football coach, has a profound conversation with an older gentleman at a local high school in Georgia. This older, godly saint tells the story of two farmers, both needing rain for their fields after experiencing a drought. After praying for the much-needed rain for their fields, one of the farmers prepared his field to receive the rain. The other did not. The question is then posed, "When the rains came—which farmer had trusted God to send it?" The answer: the one who prepared for it.

By faith, we prepare to receive what God has promised. David Pawson, a famous evangelist from England, states that, "Faith is something you do, not something you say." Pawson asked a live audience a simple question. "Do you believe in me?" A few people raised their hands. "Now," Pawson continued, "what if I asked you if you believed I existed?" The whole auditorium responded by raising their hands.[84]

The clear parallel is our attitude toward God. The first question requires more than an acknowledgment of His existence. It requires that we know Him as our Father, Creator, and Best Friend. "We do something to show that we trust God."[85] The great role call in Hebrews 11 is a list of ways Abraham, Isaac, and Jacob *acted* in the face of God's promises...treating things that are not yet as though they are already.

We must be ready, so that when God presents the opportunity, we are ready to receive it. This means preparing our hearts to receive His

Word, to receive His best for us, to receive our mate, His gentle rebuke, or His promotion. In the natural circumstances, as in the days of Noah, it may not have looked like rain. But according to Mike Bickle, "The boat makes no sense until the rain starts."[86]

God prepared Joseph's heart in exile and prison, removing any bitterness, so that he could, with confidence in God, step into a position God had planned in advance for him. When Joseph revealed his identity to his brothers, his heart response was:

> Do not be grieved or angry with yourselves, because you sold me here, for God sent me before you to preserve life. For the famine has been in the land these two years…God sent me before you to preserve for you a remnant in the earth, and to keep you alive by a great deliverance. Now, therefore, it was not you who sent me here, but God.
> —Gen. 45:5-7

It was God's desire to save the people by sending Joseph ahead into Egypt. His character was formed as he waited, and his heart was prepared for the promises God had in store. God entrusted him with a great deal; it was His plan. My question is this: what can be done in your life to prepare for rain?

> Whatever you do whether in word or deed, do all in the name of the Lord Jesus, giving thanks through Him to God the Father.
> —Col. 3:17

Chapter 24

The Finish Line

I press on toward the goal for the prize of the upward call of God in
Christ Jesus.

—Phil. 3:14

RUNNING THE RACE

PAUL SPEAKS IN Philippians about running the race with perseverance. He also speaks of running in a race to win a prize that far surpasses
the Olympic Games. For runners in that race sought after a wreath that
was perishable, but we seek an imperishable one (see 1 Cor. 9:25). Yet
our race is also different, for we are not racing against each other, but
rather, we are each running our leg of the race in our own lane, focused
on the prize.

Much as the runners who pass the baton, we have been passed the
baton for our leg of the race. Abraham, Isaac, Jacob, Noah, Moses,
Joseph, and others successfully ran their lap of the race. They were
entrusted with the baton and they carried it faithfully. Now we are
running our lap with them cheering us on in the stands.

I can imagine the apostle Paul shouting, "Go! Go to the nations!
God will give you strength to do it!" Or Moses saying, "Be brave and
daring. Be wise with your time." David declaring: "Run with a heart
after God! Give Him your whole heart. And if you stumble and fall along

the way, remember to get up and go to Him. Give Him your love, ask His forgiveness and cleansing and follow hard after Him. Don't give up! He loves weak and broken vessels yielded to Him. He loves you. Never forget that."

And Joshua shouting: "When things look impossible and the odds outrageous, that's when God shows up to show Himself faithful! That's when He is glorified, because only He could have seen you through. But He wants you to partner with Him. Be obedient and *believe* in Him, His love and promises. 'All things are possible to him who believes!'"

And Noah wisely saying, "Build the boat! Just trust me! All the heckling will be worth it! Doing His will is the ultimate! If He entrusts you with part of His heart, cherish it. You may even see its fulfillment in your lifetime. But trust me on this one; build the boat."

Isaac encouraging, "The wife He has chosen for you is His best. Pursue her, love her, and cherish her. Know that she is God's best for you!"

And Abraham, "The promises of God are true, tried, and tested. When He asks you to follow Him, you may not know exactly what to expect, but He will surprise you with more than you could have hoped for. Just *believe!*"

I think of some of the ladies who are rejoicing from heaven with us and whose lives testify to God's goodness in their lives. Saints like Elizabeth, who gave birth to John the Baptist, might say. "I was old, past childbearing, and He gave me a son. A son, who one day would rise up and call me blessed. A son, who would prepare the way for Yeshua."

Or Sarah, who gave birth in her nineties to the son that God had promised. "I laughed," she might say, "I did not take Him seriously at first. I mean I was ninety! But then, who am I to wrestle with the One who breathed…and gave life?"

And Hannah, "God heard my cry, and He answered me! He gave me the son I longed for, and I, in turn, gave him back to the Lord. And after that He gave me my heart's desire—He gave me five more children!"

All the paths of the Lord are lovingkindness and truth to those who keep His covenant.

—Ps. 25:10

My Cheerleaders

> Waiting times are growing and learning times. As you quiet your heart, you enter His peace…as you sense your weakness, you receive His strength…**as you lay down your will, you hear His calling**.
>
> —Roy Lessin

Since I was a child, my grandparents sowed into me the love and knowledge that I was treasured and special. One of the things my grandpa, or "Pops" as we affectionately called him, said to me often was, "No matter what you do in this life, Joy, we will always love you…unconditionally." Although this was difficult for me to grasp as a little girl, as I look back, I see those seeds planted early countered any lies that came later.

With my mother having four of us in a row, Grandma and Pops provided the necessary reprieve and so much more. Pops was a gem. Generous with his time, he played endless games of cribbage, cards, pool, or put puzzles together with all of us. Meanwhile, Saturday mornings were filled with cartoons and as much sugared cereal as our little hearts desired. We ate, rose on that sugar high, and crashed at Grandma's. It was fun for a day, but I am also thankful Mom fed us healthy, nutritious food all week. I never had a tooth cavity until later in life.

My grandparents were my cheerleaders. No matter what I did, they encouraged and praised me. Whenever I had a hair-brained scheme, Grandma always went along with it if she deemed it wise. Buying chocolates, pizzas, and trinkets she didn't need to help me go on a trip to Russia or Europe to sing with concert choir was just one act of her profound love. Whatever I was involved in, she actively supported. Once, I asked if we could host a carnival for kids on her front porch to raise money for MS. Grandma was all for it!

We pulled out all of her old games: bean bag toss, horseshoes, tic-tac-toe and others from the attic. Then we gave away small prizes from Nelson's Dime Store to the winners. The result was a gross of over one hundred dollars…an enormous sum to me at that time.

And then, we did the unforgettable. We drove to the phone center for our area during the telethon and presented that money to the people. Giving was a natural gift for Grandma. To this day, I am not sure how much of that money was actually hers to add on to what we had already taken in.

Another one of my favorite memories was presenting summer plays in our neighborhood. Vicki Siefert's backyard, newly paved with a basketball court, served as a stage. We hung sheets on the clothesline and sold lemonade and other concessions. After the crowd packed into the grassy area, the curtains parted, and there we were: performing four plays based on Disney movies or adaptations of our favorite stories. With colorful, cardboard backdrops that the boys painted, we were ready to go!

Hunting through Grandma's closet was like unearthing a treasure chest, as we discovered costumes from the 40s on into the present time in mint condition. Seeing my sister dress up in seventies, lime green platform shoes with a crazy, colorful dress, is etched in my memory. In fact, most of my costumes for high school theatre scene work came from Grandma's attic or downstairs closet.

My grandfather was equally loving, but in a different way. He was always willing to take time to enjoy life with you. I remember his suggestion of "shoveling the snow," which served as a ruse to get me to McDonald's with him for a Happy Meal. Sliding across the cool, vinyl seats in the middle of winter, we escaped the notice of my brothers and sister. Then, we spent time bonding over a hamburger, strawberry sundae, and fries (several of which I stole from his plate by distracting him with a, "Look, there's Ronald McDonald").

The two of them took me to get my hair permed (a process that took three hours), clipped every newspaper article about me, and always reminded me of how proud they were of me. Even in college, I found myself calling them to share news of what was going on. No matter what I said, the response was always the same. "We are so happy for you, Joy! And so proud of you too! We love you so very much."

I miss them. When I think of whom to call for encouragement or to share a surprising event, my fingers often wish to

> And I will follow the Lamb. I will follow that Man wherever He goes.
> *Dana Candler*

place a very long distance phone call. This time it would be to heaven, where both of them now graciously reside. I can imagine them, beaming as they gaze down at me and then at each other, smiling and saying, "We are so proud of you, Joy. And we love you very much."

> Therefore, since we have so great a cloud of witnesses surrounding us, let us also lay aside every encumbrance and the sin which so easily entangles us, and let us run with endurance the race that is set before us, fixing our eyes on Jesus, the author and perfecter of faith.
> —Heb. 12:1-2

Endnotes

1. Dana Candler, *Awakened to Love*. Women in the Prophetic Conference, International House of Prayer (IHOP), 2005.
2. E.M. Bounds, *Answered Prayer* (New Kensington, PA: Whitaker house, 1994), 60.
3. John Gill. "Commentary on Acts 8:39". *The New John Gill Exposition of the Entire Bible*. <http://www.studylight.org/com/geb/view.cgi?book=ac and chapter=008 and verse=039>. 1999.
4. Stuart Greaves, *Pursuing Christ-Centered Social Justice*. One Thing Conference, IHOP, 2008.
5. John Gill. "Commentary on Numbers 13:20". *The New John Gill Exposition of the Entire Bible*. <http://www.studylight.org/com/geb/view.cgi?book=nu and chapter=013 and verse=020>. 1999.
6. "Numbers 13: Twelve Men Sent To Search Out The Land of Canaan," *Matthew Henry's Concise Commentary*. <http://www.biblegateway.com/resources/commentaries/index.php?action=getCommentaryText and cid=21 and source=2 and seq=i.4.13.1>
7. Rick Warren, *The Purpose Driven Life* (Grand Rapids, MI: Zondervan, 2002), 25.
8. Dutch Sheets, *Intercessory Prayer: How God Can Use Your Prayers to Move Heaven and Earth* (Ventura, CA: Regal Books, 1996), 50.
9. Ibid.

10. C. Peter Wagner, *Prayer Shield* (Ventura, CA: Regal Books, 1992), 268.

11. Ibid., 29.

12. Lou Giglio, *Indescribable Tour* (Brentwood, TN: Sparrow Records, 2008).

13. Ibid.

14. "Theology: Who Is God?" *The Truth Project* (Colorado Springs, CO: Focus on the Family, 2007).

15. Michael Behe, *The Case for a Creator* (Illustra Media, 2006).

16. Stephen Meyer, Ph.D, *Unlocking the Mystery of Life* (Illustra Media, 2006).

17. Jed Macosko, Ph.D, *Unlocking the Mystery of Life* (Illustra Media, 2006).

18. Lou Giglio, *Indescribable Tour* (Brentwood, TN: Sparrow Records, 2008).

19. Lee Strobel, *The Case for a Creator* (Illustra Media, 2006).

20. Professor Gary Goldstein and Marvin Sherwin, *The Nuclear Age: Its Physics and History.* Physics 5, Spring 1998. http://www.tufts.edu/as/physics/courses/physics5/estim_97.html.

21. E.M. Bounds, *Answered Prayer* "(New Kensington, PA: Whitaker House, 1994), 85.

22. Jack Hayford, *A New Time and Place: Preparing Yourself to Receive God's Best* (Nashville, TN: Thomas Nelson Publishers, 1996), 128.

23. Jackie Kendall and Debby Jones, *Lady in Waiting: Becoming God's Best While Waiting for Mr. Right,* (Shippensburg, PA: Destiny Image Publishers, Inc, 2005), 95.

24. Kent Hovind, "The Age of the Earth," *The Creation Series.* (Arden, NC: Christian Films, 2007).

25. E.M. Bounds, *Answered Prayer* (New Kensington, PA: Whitaker House, 1994), 85.

26. Mike Bickle, *Song of Songs* (Kansas City, MO: Forerunner Music, 2000).

27. John Gill, "Commentary on Song of Solomon 4:12." *The New John Gill Exposition of the Entire Bible.* <http://www.studylight.org/com/geb/view.cgi?book=so andand chapter=004 andand verse=012>. 1999.

28. Ibid.

29. James Orr, M.A., D.D. General Editor, "Entry for 'SPIKENARD'". *International Standard Bible Encyclopedia.* <http://www.studylight. org/enc/isb/view.cgi?number=T8335>. 1915.

30. John Gill. "Commentary on Song of Solomon 4:12". *The New John Gill Exposition of the Entire Bible.* <http://www.studylight.org/com/ geb/view.cgi?book=so and chapter=004 and verse=012>. 1999.

31. Ibid.

32. Ibid.

33. Thayer and Smith. "Greek Lexicon entry for Metanoeo". *The New Testament Greek Lexicon.* <http://www.studylight.org/lex/grk/view. cgi?number=3340>.

34. John and Stasi Eldredge, *Captivating* (New York, NY: Thomas Nelson, 2005).

35. Ibid.

36. Dr. Dell Tackett, *The Truth Project.* (Colorado Springs, CO: Focus on the Family, 2006.)

37. Misty Edwards, *IHOP Limited Edition* (Kansas City, MO: Forerunner Music, 2006).

38. Alan Hood, *One Thing Conference 2008* (Kansas City, MO: IHOP, 2008).

39. Mike Bickle, *Song of Solomon* (Kansas City: Forerunner Publishing, 2000).

40. Ibid.

41. Dana Candler, *Awakened to Love.* Women in the Prophetic Conference, IHOP, 2005.

42. Mike Bickle, *Passion for Jesus* (Lake Mary, FL: Charisma House, 1993).

43. "Nardoi," *Matthew Henry's Concise Commentary.* <<http://www. biblegateway.com/resources/commentaries/?action=getCommentary Text and cid=51 and source=2 and seq=i.50.12.1>

44. John Gill. "Commentary on Acts 7:56". *The New John Gill Exposition of the Entire Bible.* <http://www.studylight.org/com/geb/view. cgi?book=ac and chapter=007 and verse=056>. 1999.

45. "Greek Term for 'Peter," *Hitchcock's Bible Names Dictionary.* http:// www.biblegateway.com/resources/dictionaries.

46. Jack Hayford, *A New Time and Place: Preparing Yourself to Receive God's Best* (Nashville, TN: Thomas Nelson Publishers, 1996), 48.
47. Ibid., 128.
48. Mike Bickle, *The Seven Churches of Revelation*, (Kansas City, MO: Forerunner School of Ministry, 2008), 19.
49. Ibid.
50. "Asherim," *Interlinear Study Bible.* http://www.studylight.org/isb/bible.cgi?query=asherim and section=0 and it=nas andoq=asherim andot=bhs andnt=na andnew=1.
51. Mike Bickle, *Passion for Jesus*, p. 24.
52. Ibid.
53. Jacinta Bronte-Tinkew, "The Father-Child Relationship, Parenting Styles, and Adolescent Risk Behaviors in Intact Families" *Journal of Family Issues,* vol. 27, Number 6. June, 2006. Page(s) 850-881.
54. Ibid.
55. John and Paula Sanford, *Healing the Wounded Spirit*, (South Plainfield: Bridge Publishers, Inc, 1985), 40-42.
56. Albert Barnes. "Commentary on Matthew 18". *Barnes' Notes on the New Testament.* <http://www.studylight.org/com/bnn/view.cgi?book=mt and chapter=018>
57. A.T. Robertson "Commentary on Matthew 18:24". *Robertson's Word Pictures of the New Testament.* <http://www.studylight.org/com/rwp/view.cgi?book=mt and chapter=018 and verse=024>. (Broadman Press 1932,33, Renewal 1960).
58. Thayer and Smith. "Greek Lexicon entry for charis". *The New Testament Greek Lexicon.*
59. Thayer and Smith. "Greek Lexicon entry for Ergon". *The New Testament Greek Lexicon.* <http://www.studylight.org/lex/grk/view.cgi?number=2041>.
60. Phillip Keller, *A Shepherd Looks at Psalm 23* (Grand Rapids, MI: Zondervan, 1970), 51-52.
61. Ibid., 53.
62. Floyd, McClung, *The Father Heart of God: Experiencing the Depths of His Love for You* (Eugene, OR: Harvest House Publishers, 1985), 77.
63. Ibid.

64. "Beautiful Gate," *Easton's 1897 Bible Dictionary*. <http://www.biblegateway.com/resources/dictionaries/dict_meaning.php?source=1 and wid=T0000492>

65. "The Healing of the Crippled Beggar," *IVP New Testament Commentary*. Intervarsity Press. <http://www.biblegateway.com/resources/commentaries/index.php?action=getCommentaryText and cid=5 and source=1 and seq=i.51.3.3>

66. "A Lame Man Healed By Peter and John," *Matthew Henry's Concise Commentary* <http://www.biblegateway.com/resources/commentaries/index.php?action=getCommentaryText and cid=52 and source=2 and seq=i.51.3.1>

67. John Gill. "Commentary on Luke 8:47". "The New John Gill Exposition of the Entire Bible". <http://www.studylight.org/com/geb/view.cgi?book=lu and chapter=008 and verse=047>. 1999.

68. John Gill. "Commentary on Matthew 8:9". *The New John Gill Exposition of the Entire Bible*. <http://www.studylight.org/com/geb/view.cgi?book=mt and chapter=008 and verse=008>. 1999.

69. Ibid.

70. Neil T. Andersen, *The Common Made Holy* (Eugene, OR: Harvest House Publishers, 1997).

71. Chester and Betsy Kylstra, *Restoring the Foundations* (Santa Rosa Beach, FL: Proclaiming His Word Ministries, 2000).

72. Mike Bickle, *Passion for Jesus*, 68-69.

73. Corey Russell, *One Thing 2008 Conference* (Kansas City, MO: IHOP, 2008).

74. Dr. Jim Baessler, Ph.D. "Interview." Old Dominion University, June 2, 2006.

75. R.T. Kendall, *Total Forgiveness* (Lake Mary, FL: Charisma House, 2002).

76 David Pawson, "The Five Covenants of Scripture," *IHOPU Seminar With David Pawson*, March 21, 2009.

77. Ibid.

78. Chris Cunningham, Ph.D. "Here Come the Anointed Ones." New Life Providence Church, February 23, 2009.

79. Ibid.

80. Daniel S. Lim, *The Wise Virgins*, (Kansas City, MO: Forerunner, March 8, 2009).

81. *Creation Tips: Answers on Evolution, Creation Science, Genesis and the Bible.* <http://www.creationtips.com/arksize.html>

82. Interview, *Evan Almighty*.

83. Kent Hovind, "The Age of the Earth," *The Creation Series*. (Arden, NC: Christian Films, 2007).

84. David Pawson, "The Five Covenants of Scripture," *IHOPU Seminar with David Pawson*, March 21, 2009.

85. Ibid.

86. Mike Bickle, (Kansas City, MO: Forerunner Publishing, 2009).

WinePressPublishing
Great Books, Defined.

To order additional copies of this book call:
1-877-421-READ (7323)
or please visit our website at
www.WinePressbooks.com

If you enjoyed this quality custom-published book,
drop by our website for more books and information.

www.winepresspublishing.com
"Your partner in custom publishing."

CPSIA information can be obtained at www.ICGtesting.com
Printed in the USA
BVOW022002160712

295375BV00002B/18/P